LADY DAY
REVELATIONS

David Pinner
LADY DAY
REVELATIONS

OBERON BOOKS
LONDON

First published in 2003 by Oberon Books Ltd.
(incorporating Absolute Classics)
521 Caledonian Road, London N7 9RH
Tel: 020 7607 3637 / Fax: 020 7607 3629

e-mail: oberon.books@btinternet.com
www.oberonbooks.com

A catalogue record for this book is available from the British
Library.

ISBN: 1 84002 385 6

Cover design: Andrzej Klimowski

Printed in Great Britain by Antony Rowe Ltd, Chippenham.

Contents

Preface

I wrote four plays in the series *Seasons* over several years, focusing on mankind's relationship with nature. The plays explore the need for belief systems and their attendant seasonal rituals. *Lady Day* (winter) set beside a frozen lake, charts the bizarre fortunes of a defiant woman who leaves her home comforts to return to nature in the darkest season of the year. *Revelations* (spring) is set on a storm-torn cliff top and a moonlit beach, and follows the tortuous destiny of a stranger who does not believe in God, but who is viewed by a desperate, isolated village as a modern messiah, with disturbing consequences. *Midsummer* (summer), set on a sunlit lawn, in a garden at dawn and a midnight wood, is a contemporary homage to Shakespeare's *A Midsummer Night's Dream*, evoking pantheistic magic and the desire to be bewitched and transformed. *All Hallows' Eve* (autumn), set in a leaf-strewn library-cum-music room, is a psychological ghost story exploring one of the great taboos.

At the beginning of my comedy *Lady Day*, the forty-year-old Katya discovers that her husband, Steve, is having an affair with her best friend, Judith. Katya's reaction is drastic. She ups and leaves the relative comfort of her home, and decides to 'hibernate' in a dilapidated, unheated lake-side cottage in freezing December so she can commune with nature. In order to re-discover her identity she insists on being challenged by the rawness of wildlife around the lake. She embraces various winter rituals of light that were practiced by her pre-Christian forefathers to illuminate the darkest season of the year.

Katya's family and friends accuse her of being insane. They cannot accept the idea that she no longer needs them, and that she prefers to live alone, save for the companionship of the owls, foxes and a trillion stars. As her loved ones frenziedly attempt to prise Katya away from her icy lakeside vigil, they use every weapon at their disposal, including lust, blackmail and self-denigration. But they, in turn, are forced to come to terms with the potency of nature and the hostile elements.

This soon blossoms into farcical mayhem when all the men in Katya's life fall in love with her simultaneously. Then all the women in her life beg Katya to release all their men. On Lady Day, 25 March, Katya comes up with a bizarre solution. She provokes the men to have a multiple duel with swords and pistols to determine who is going to possess her. The play's climax is comically anarchic as the 'lady' finally has her 'day', and the last say.

From the moment I read W B Yeats' *The Second Coming*, I wanted to write about a modern messiah. Or, more accurately, I envisaged creating a play about a man who is considered to be a modern messiah by a group of villagers who find themselves in a state of spiritual, mental and physical extremis. I wrote *Revelations* after visiting the desolate remains of a cliff-top village in Devon, some of which can still be seen under the waves. As a result of a terrible storm in the 1920s, the cliff gave way and most of the village fell into the sea.

Revelations is set in an isolated fishing village on the bleak 'east coast of anywhere' in the wake of a storm that causes life-threatening fissures to appear under all the houses on the crumbling cliff top. The villagers' desperation is compounded by severe soil erosion, an ocean which cannot be fished because it is too polluted, and the fact that the sun never shines, even though it is Spring. Then Joe, an itinerant carpenter, appears in the village, bringing the sun with him. Inadvertently Joe touches Beth, an old woman suffering with cancer, and seemingly her cancer disappears. Other apparent 'miracles' follow, prompting the villagers to hail Joe as a new 'Messiah'. At first Joe is amused as he doesn't believe in God. He is seduced by the villagers' flattery, and he enjoys his power without accepting responsibility for his actions. Then Jed, the local Marxist school teacher, begins to play subversive mind-games with Joe, to reassert his waning influence over the locals, and so the nightmare begins.

The play explores how people need to be led by a strong, charismatic leader. But if things start to go wrong, those very same people turn on the leader and pillory him – or worse. In *Revelations* I examine the complex reactions to the idea of 'miracles'. During this present age, in our so-called civilised society, what – or who – are we willing to kill for? And is there anything left we are willing to die for?

LADY DAY

a comedy

Characters

STEVE

JUDITH

DON
Judith's husband

PIPA
Steve's daughter

MARK
Pipa's boyfriend

KATYA
Steve's wife

ACT ONE

Scene 1

A wood in the Home Counties.

Time: the present. 1 December. A chilly afternoon.

Between fir trees, we can make out the corner of a workman's cottage, including one window and the front door. The cottage, built during Cromwell's Protectorate, is boarded up and desolate.

There is a small, dilapidated, wooden lean-to next to the cottage. The wood and its undergrowth have all but obliterated the cottage garden.

An ancient, stunted apple tree, with half a dozen leaves, and some windswept bulrushes overhang the small lake – in which the audience is sitting.

Shafts of wintry sunlight lance down on the water. Wind keens in the trees. A blackbird sings.

STEVE who is lean, bearded and in his forties, strides into view. He is a no-nonsense Lancastrian who is overtly proud of his bluntness. As always he is wearing his old, dusty builder's coat.

JUDITH and her husband, DON, bring up the rear. JUDITH is a lissom, raunchy, mink-coated and mink-hatted New Yorker in her late thirties. While DON (the same age), swaddled in his London School of Economics scarf and battered black overcoat, is an overweight pleb from Clacton-on-Sea who looks habitually miserable.

All three are weighed down with picnic hampers, bulging carrier bags, deckchairs and cushions. STEVE carries a folding table. They come to a complaining halt under the apple tree.

The wind keens on. The blackbird stops singing.

The trio stare at the boarded-up cottage, then at the lake, and then at each other. In unison they drop everything they are carrying.

Shaking his head in disbelief STEVE starts to assemble the table while DON unfolds the chairs.

STEVE: I still say Katya's cracked. Completely cracked.
(*JUDITH unwraps a veritable banquet of goodies.*)

JUDITH: Oh c'mon, Stevo, there's no saner woman in these godforsaken isles than your wife. (*Shivering with cold.*) Most of the time.

STEVE: (*Watching her lay the table.*) If she isn't cracked, then why the hell does she want us to have a picnic here on the First of December? This wind'll cut us in half and it's bound to bloody snow!

DON: (*Indicating the derelict cottage as he lights his pipe.*) This was built during Cromwell's Protectorate, wasn't it?
(*DON wanders round behind the cottage.*)

STEVE: (*Now wrestling with an obstinate deckchair.*) Ay, and it badly needs renovating, but I've not had the time to go near it. Damn near two years since we've moved down here, and our house in the village is still in a shambles.
(*STEVE howls with pain as he traps his finger in the deckchair. JUDITH laughs. Snarling STEVE finally assembles the deckchair and slumps into it. Instantly the chair breaks up under him, throwing STEVE onto his back.*)
Oh scrotum!

JUDITH: (*Laughing.*) I think it's more likely to be woodworm.
(*Painfully STEVE extricates himself from the broken deckchair.*)

STEVE: Nobody but a fully paid-up nutter has a picnic in winter. (*Whirling the deckchair round his head.*) Why does everything betray me?

JUDITH: (*Assessing the banquet.*) Fish paté with paprika, tomato-and-onion quiche, cocktail sausages and lentils, game-pie, sherry trifle and three bottles of Alsace Sylvaner. Katya's certainly outdone herself this time.
(*STEVE storms out of view with the deckchair.*)
Where are you going?

STEVE: (*Off.*) To deal with this heap of crap.
(*DON materialises from behind the cottage.*)

DON: (*Calling after him.*) Don't throw yourself in the lake, Steve. Remember Judith can't swim, and I can't jump in and rescue you 'cause I'm a politician.

(*DON dips his finger in the paté. JUDITH slaps his wrist. Off, there is a resounding splash. PIP (STEVE's attractive nineteen-year-old daughter) comes in, holding hands with her boyfriend MARK (twenty), who is bespectacled and has a Cockney accent.*)

PIP: Hi, Judith.

JUDITH: Oh hi, Pip. Your father has just...

PIP: ...Chucked his deckchair in the lake, I know.

JUDITH: (*To DON.*) Hunbun, you have met Pip's latest beau, haven't you?

DON: (*Nodding.*) 'Mark', isn't it?

MARK: (*Extending his hand.*) Yes, Mr er...?

(*Oblivious to MARK's proffered hand, DON subsides into a chair.*)

DON: Kant. Spelt with an 'a'.

(*DON produces a bottle of white liquid from his overcoat pocket and swigs half the contents. MARK looks on in amazement.*)

JUDITH: (*To MARK.*) Milk, honey. For his ulcer. Politician's trademark.

MARK: Oh, are you an MP, then, Mr Kant?

DON: On and off.

MARK: I see. (*Which he doesn't.*) Which er...side are you on?

DON: Varies.

MARK: Yes, of course it would do...

(*STEVE re-appears.*)

Oh hello, Mr Wendover. Is Mrs Wendover joining us?

STEVE: God knows. (*Digging a fork into the lentils.*) Well, as it's all laid out, folks, and there's no sign of the hostess, we might as well get stuck in.

PIP: (*Shivering.*) Bit chilly for a picnic, isn't it?

STEVE: (*Ladling food onto his plate.*) Freeze your goolies off.

PIP: Dad! Mark's not used to your kind of vulgarity.

STEVE: (*To MARK.*) In the food business, ent you, lad?

MARK: Yes, as a matter of fact I am, Mr Wendover.

17

STEVE: I'd've thought anyone who works in a supermarket on a day to day basis would find my language rather too refined.

(*DON burps, groans and finishes his milk.*)

JUDITH: Don't just sit there milking your cow, Farmer Giles. Open the booze.

(*JUDITH throws DON a corkscrew. PIP piles food onto her plate while STEVE re-fills his. Tentatively MARK helps himself.*)

STEVE: Get shovelling, laddie. My wife's a lousy cook but you can only snuff it once.

PIP: Dad's right about her cooking. For the last couple of weeks Mum's served us nothing but herring paté, lentils and stewed prunes.

STEVE: Yeah, and most of the time she slops 'em all on the same bleeding plate!

DON: (*Pulling out the wine cork with a great effort.*) Jesus, I think I've given myself a hernia.

STEVE: Ugh! This is last night's fish paté.

MARK: How'd you know?

STEVE: Just swallowed a sodding prune! Mind, I could cope with her rotten cooking if she didn't spend the rest of her time re-reading the life of Emily Dickinson.

JUDITH: Emily Dickinson didn't have a life.

STEVE: Exactly.

MARK: (*Pointing at the lake.*) Wasn't that a kingfisher?

DON: No. Just a shadow on the water. (*Pointing.*) That is a swan, though.

STEVE: (*Helping himself to dessert.*) Where the bleeding hell is she, anyway?

JUDITH: Perhaps she's still at the Library.

PIP: Mum never works on Sunday afternoons. She didn't even when we lived in East Sheen.

STEVE: (*Spitting food out.*) Yuck! The trifle's got prunes in it, too. What the devil's Katya playing at? I'm supposed to be installing a new staircase in our house, not freezing my goolies off at her farcical picnic.

JUDITH: You got cream in your beard, Stevie-pooh.

(*PIP laughs.*)

STEVE: You may well snigger, Pipa, but time is money in the building trade. And I'm puke-sick of working my guts out all week, converting some rich bastard's Victorian eye-sore into the Brighton Pavilion, and then having to spend every godawful weekend putting in a damp course, re-tiling and re-plastering in our own rotten house – while your nutty mother does nothing but devour Emily Dickinson and the Russian Classics, or ponces about for hours in these woods bird-spotting with my Japanese binoculars. Well, I ask you – is it fair?

DON: No, I think it's clouding over. (*Pouring wine for the others.*) Anyway, whatever you say about your wife, she's certainly different.

STEVE: You should try living with her sometime, mate.

DON: If only, if only.

STEVE: You serious?

JUDITH: 'Course he isn't. Are you, hunbunch?

DON: No. Unfortunately. Once a Puritan, always a voyeur.

PIP: Mum's bound to have a good reason for being late.

DON: Yes, for all we know Katya's out there somewhere saving the nation.

MARK: Saving the nation?

DON: It certainly needs saving. Our castrated democracy has reached an impasse.

JUDITH: Oh don't you start, for God's sake.

DON: It's true. No one believes in the soul anymore, or morality. (*Enjoying the sound of his own voice.*) Everywhere you lurch, the Plastic Divinities hold sway; Lethargy, Negativity, Hypocrisy and Pornography, not to mention Sadism, Masochism, Cynicism, Nihilism, Defeatism, Anarchism and New Wanking Labour!

JUDITH: Don, for Chrissakes, hush up, will you? You've lost your seat in the Commons. So why don't you give your ulcer a rest and take another swig on your teat?

DON: (*Producing another bottle of milk from his coat pocket.*) I'm fully aware that I'm not in the House anymore, Judith, but I still have the misfortune to lecture at the LSE. And if you had to teach a bunch of nose-picking nitwits the political facts of life every working day of the week, you'd find that you'd be spouting off like a demented whale, too.

JUDITH: (*Shouting back.*) Listen, buster, year in year out I work my ass off in that stinking Bureau trying to find nice, cushy jobs for your nose-picking layabouts, so don't give me all that whining academic shit!

STEVE: (*Throwing down his empty plate.*) I've had this picnic up to here. And as most of the grub's gone, I'm off.

JUDITH: Think I'll join you. (*To DON.*) Coming, milk chops?

DON: (*Shaking his head.*) I'm going to stay on for a bit and listen to the lake.

STEVE: You feeling alright, wac?

DON: (*Smiling.*) No.

(*STEVE and JUDITH exchange looks.*)

(*Pointing over the lake.*) I wouldn't mind being that swan for a day or two. Must be so soothing out there, alone, riding on the water. Then serenely watching your own reflection...all white and shimmering in the lake's undulating darkness.

(*Again STEVE and JUDITH exchange looks.*)

STEVE: Yes, well, Don, when you eventually sign yourself into the local booby-hutch alongside my dear wife, do give her my love, won't you?

DON: With pleasure, Steve. Truth is, I wish I had the guts to follow Katya's 'insane' example, and rethink my life.

JUDITH: (*Lighting a cigarette.*) Oh c'mon, dumdum, nobody rethinks their lives. When you reach our age, you have to make do with the shit you're lumbered with. So even if you do make the occasional New Year's resolution and diligently try to carry it out, by Lady Day you'll find yourself right back where you were.

MARK: Where's that, Mrs Kant?

JUDITH: (*Puffing on her cigarette.*) Up to your neck in the same over-flowing ash tray. (*To DON.*) So forget it, honey.

Whatever surface contortions you put yourself through, you can never really change yourself.

(*Off, we hear a woman's voice: 'I hope to Heaven that you're wrong, Judith. For all our sakes.' Moments later, the broken deckchair lands at JUDITH's feet.*)

What the hell?

(*KATYA, an attractive forty-five year-old, saunters into view, in a low-cut summer dress and a becoming floppy straw hat. She is pushing a green wheelbarrow, covered by a dust-sheet, on top of which is perched her large white handbag.*)

STEVE: About bloody time and all!

KATYA: (*Smiling.*) What a perfect day for a picnic.

STEVE: Where the hell've you been, Katya? And why are you undressed like that? You'll catch your death, woman.

KATYA: Nonsense; when one is elated, there's no such thing as a goosebump. Even if one is moderately panic-stricken.

STEVE: Turning up this late, you should be a damn sight more than 'panic-stricken'.

DON: Don't take any notice of him, Katya. You look absolutely stunning.

KATYA: (*Smiling.*) 'Thank you, kind sir,' she said.

(*KATYA wheels the barrow towards the cottage.*)

PIP: What've you got in the barrow, Mum?

(*With a flourish, KATYA removes the dust sheet to reveal a barrowload of…*)

KATYA: Books, dear.

JUDITH: (*Examining a book.*) All on Emily Dickinson?

KATYA: (*Amused.*) Unfortunately not. Most of them are Russian Classics.

STEVE: (*Picking up the broken deck chair.*) As I said – she's completely cracked.

MARK: What are you going to do with that?

STEVE: Chuck it back where it belongs, of course.

(*STEVE marches off with the deckchair.*)

KATYA: Funny man.

(*KATYA starts to unload the books from the barrow onto the front step of the cottage.*)

JUDITH: (*Watching KATYA and shaking her head.*) Everyone's gone completely nuts.

(*KATYA drops a book. MARK rushes forward to retrieve it.*)

MARK: Can I be of any assistance, Mrs Wendover?

KATYA: I must say it's very reassuring to find that there are still pockets of gallantry in the Home Counties.

DON: (*Levering himself out of his chair with his customary groan.*) Katya, let me give you a hand with those.

KATYA: My goodness, do I actually see a politician standing for something?

DON: Cut the quips and tell us where you want this lot stacked.

(*KATYA unlocks the cottage and indicates a table inside.*)

KATYA: The table's as good a place as any, thank you.

(*DON helps MARK take the books into the cottage. Off, there is a huge splash.*)

JUDITH: You don't think Big Stevo's jumped in the lake, do you?

KATYA: I certainly hope so. He needs to cool down.

(*STEVE returns, minus the deckchair.*)

PIP: You didn't throw the chair in the lake again.

STEVE: Damn right I did. What's more, I God near sank a sodding swan.

JUDITH: (*Pointedly folding her arms.*) Speaking personally, I've had about as much of this mad house as I can take.

KATYA: Didn't you enjoy my picnic?

JUDITH: Enjoy it!?

KATYA: Obviously someone did because there's only a helping of trifle left – (*Spooning some trifle onto a plate.*) – which is a bit of a shame as I'm rather peckish.

PIP: Mum, why have you laid on a picnic in the middle of winter?

KATYA: (*Savouring her trifle.*) I thought it would provide an amusing climax.

STEVE: To what?

KATYA: (*Sampling her trifle.*) If you don't know, Stephen, no one does.

JUDITH: Look, what the devil's all this about, Katya?

KATYA: (*Smiling.*) Something rather…diabolical. (*To MARK and DON, who have finished stacking the books in the cottage.*) Thank you, gentlemen, you've been most helpful.

PIP: Where've you been all this time, Mum?

KATYA: Packing, dear.

STEVE: Packing?

KATYA: I'm leaving you, Stephen. (*Discarding her trifle with a smile.*) Won't be a sec.

(*KATYA goes off.*)

STEVE: Leaving me?! (*Shouting after her.*) You can't do this to me! Katya, come back here this instant. I said come back here! (*To the others.*) I'm not running after her. She'll regret all her loony antics when she's had time to think about it.

(*STEVE's ranting is interrupted by the sound of a large van bumping towards them through the undergrowth.*)

Where the hell did she get that van from?

PIP: God knows. She must've hidden it in the bushes.

(*The van stops, then goes into reverse.*)

Whatever does Mum think she's up to?

STEVE: (*Concerned.*) She isn't about to elope with some bloke, is she?

JUDITH: Her chief librarian's pretty cute. In a hairy sort of way.

DON: I thought the chief librarian was a woman?

JUDITH: She is.

DON: You're not suggesting that Katya's become a lesbian, are you?

JUDITH: (*Grinning.*) We must leave no stone unturned.

(*Off, we hear the van doors being opened.*)

KATYA: (*Off.*) Mark, would you be a dear and give me a hand with these?

MARK: (*Hurrying off.*) With pleasure, Mrs Wendover.

DON: (*Following him off.*) Katya, put those down! You'll do yourself an injury.

STEVE: (*Charging off after them.*) Bloody hell, half of that's my stuff! (*As he disappears.*) Katya, take that lot back to the house at once!

(*JUDITH laughs and opens the second bottle of wine.*)

PIP: D'you think Mum's having some kind of brainstorm?

JUDITH: No, but I wouldn't be surprised if she wasn't planning to give us one.

STEVE: (*Off, shouting.*) Leggo of that, Don! That's my suitcase! And the red un's mine and all.

PIP: If only Dad wasn't so predictable in his choice of colours.

(*KATYA comes into view, laden down with bedding and pillows. She is followed by STEVE who is still struggling for possession of the suitcases that DON is grimly carrying.*)

STEVE: Will you leggo of my steaming cases, Kant?

DON: No, but if you don't get out of my way, I'm going to slam 'em down on your in-growing toe-nails.

STEVE: You wouldn't dare, wac.

(*DON slams a case on STEVE's foot.*)

OOWWW! (*Cradling his foot as he hops painfully.*) You've just buggered up six'n half months of primetime chiropody!

(*DON grins and takes the cases into the cottage. KATYA collects her bedding for the cottage.*)

PIP: Where'd you get the van from, Mum?

KATYA: I hired it. Then I camouflaged it over night.

STEVE: Camouflaged it?

(*DON heads back to the van.*)

DON: (*Disappearing.*) I'll fetch some more of your stuff from the van, okay?

KATYA: Thank you, Donald.

STEVE: More?! (*Waving some bedding which he has just snatched from the cottage.*) This is my monogrammed pillowcase!

KATYA: (*Taking the pillow case from him and shaking her head.*) It's from the spare room, Stephen.

(*JUDITH is trying not to laugh as she lights another cigarette. From the wood we hear various bangings. Then MARK puffs into view, dragging a gigantic trunk behind him.*)

MARK: Talk about weighing a ton.

STEVE: (*Barring his way.*) Oh no, you don't. My Hornby train-set is in that trunk. And all my Mecano!

KATYA: Don't get your nappies in a twist, Stephen. I've laid out your train-set, your Mecano and your one-eyed teddy on *your* side of the bed, alright.
(*DON helps MARK drag the trunk into the cottage.*)
When you've finished with the trunk, Mark, perhaps you'll be kind enough to fetch the china and the Primus stove.
(*Nodding, MARK re-appears from the kitchen, and plods off with the wheelbarrow.*)

PIP: Mark, you shouldn't help Mum. It's only encouraging her.

MARK: (*Disappearing.*) I don't care. She's an absolute knockout.

KATYA: (*To PIP when MARK has gone.*) I don't know whether you've noticed, dear, but your boyfriend has such erotic eyelashes.

PIP: What?

KATYA: Instead of curling upwards as is customary, his lashes stick straight out. The Freudian implications are inescapable.
(*KATYA goes off to the van. STEVE watches her in disbelief.*)

PIP: (*Laughing.*) You should see your face, Dad.

STEVE: It's not funny! Don't just sit there smoking and smirking, Judith. Do something!

JUDITH: Such as?

STEVE: Anything! So long as it stops Crazy Jane in her tracks.
(*MARK re-appears, pushing the wheelbarrow, complete with Primus stove and a wooden crate containing assorted china. As her belongings are precariously balanced on top of one another, KATYA is supervising the operation.*)

KATYA: Now careful, dear, careful does it.
(*MARK stumbles and the teapot falls out of the barrow and smashes.*)

MARK: Oh I'm so sorry, Mrs Wendover.

KATYA: (*Picking up the teapot handle.*) Doesn't matter. It's only my Dresden teapot.

STEVE: You mean it was *my* Dresden teapot!

25

KATYA: Well, you can have the handle, Stephen, and I'll keep the spout.

(*During this, DON has gone off unnoticed. He now returns with a large box, plus a brush and dustpan.*)

DON: As Confucius once said: (*In his version of a Chinese accent.*) 'She that goes off the handle, generally has one up the spout.'

(*Everybody groans but MARK, who laughs at DON's apology for a joke. Still chortling to himself DON takes the box into the cottage. KATYA is helping MARK with the tea chest when STEVE grabs her wrist and swings her round.*)

STEVE: Look, this has gone far enough, Katya. Now take all this stuff back home where it belongs before you do something you'll permanently regret!

KATYA: (*Disengaging her wrist.*) There's only one thing I permanently regret, Stephen.

STEVE: What's that?

KATYA: I regret that I didn't do this months ago.

PIP: Didn't do what, Mum?

KATYA: Move into the cottage, of course. On my own.

JUDITH: You're not seriously thinking of living here?

KATYA: Absolutely.

STEVE: Oh c'mon, you can't possibly live in this dump.

KATYA: Why not?

STEVE: Well, for one thing; it's…well, it's full of dirty great spiders that bite.

PIP: And I've seen at least nine cockroaches.

JUDITH: And there's bound to be enough mice in there to give even Beatrice Potter the shakes.

STEVE: Not to mention glissgliss.

MARK: (*Who has come out of the cottage to collect the Primus stove.*) What's a 'glissgliss' when it's at home?

PIP: A cross between a long-tailed squirrel and a giant rat.

KATYA: That's no way to describe your father, dear.

STEVE: OOOHH!

(*Laughing KATYA follows MARK into the cottage as DON comes out to collect some more stuff from the wheelbarrow.*)

(*Barring his way.*) You've a bloody cheek, Kant. I invite

you round here for a lovely picnic in my magnificent
woods beside my swanny lake – all of which I've earned
with the sweat of my migrained brow – and what do you
do to me in return?

(*DON ignores him and goes into the cottage. STEVE follows
him.*)

(*Shouting.*) You callously shove your honking snout
between me and what's legally mine, i.e.; my lawful,
awful wife!

KATYA: (*Coming out of the cottage and sweeping past STEVE.*)
He also regards me as his ox, his ass and his moveables.
Indeed I'm little more than a curvaceous dray-horse,
only fit for ploughing – and occasionally being
ploughed.

STEVE: I'm not standing for this!

KATYA: (*Pushing STEVE into an adjacent chair.*) Then sit for
it, Stephen. (*To the others.*) And none of you should be
taken in by all his subWordsworthian guff about his
mouldy old woods and his swan-song lake because none
of this is his.

JUDITH: What?

KATYA: Oh you didn't really believe that this stockbroker's
Paradise belonged to our Stephen, did you? It belongs to
the Forestry Commission.

JUDITH: (*To STEVE.*) You lying sonovabitch.

KATYA: (*Pouring herself a glass of wine.*) And the Forestry
Commission only allows us to live here, for a nominal
rent, on condition that we substantially improve the
property. That's why Stephen spends every weekend
industriously destroying our house, and why I'm now
going to do my bit to wreck what's left of this cottage.

PIP: Mum, you still haven't told us why the hell you want
to live in this total ruin?

KATYA: You know why.

JUDITH: We don't! So why don't you stop being so
goddam elliptical and spell it out for us?

KATYA: Are you telling me that you've spent this entire
picnic discussing nothing but the London School of

Economics, Don's desire to be transmogrified into a swan and my delectable prune paté?

STEVE: How do you know that's what we discussed?

KATYA: I was particularly enamoured by your diatribe on Emily Dickinson, poncing around in the woods, searching for my Russian Classics with your Japanese binoculars. That is, of course, once I'd recovered from the culture shock.

JUDITH: You've been spying on us!

KATYA: (*Smiling.*) More a case of playing hostess at a discreet distance.

(*KATYA produces a pair of binoculars from her handbag.*)

STEVE: (*Snatching the binoculars from KATYA.*) I told you she'd nabbed my Jap binocs!

KATYA: (*As MARK and DON's bemused faces appear in the doorway.*) All in all, it was a memorable experience, seeing your querulous little quintet in close-up while I practised my lip-reading.

DON: Where were you hiding?

KATYA: Behind that phallic pine tree.

(*STEVE chokes on his wine. KATYA smiles at JUDITH.*)

I find fir trees are so vibrantly masculine. You should try pressing yourself against a giant pine sometime, Judith. It's an instant turn-on. The trunk is so long and firm and straight and strong and very barky. It makes most men seem positively limp. In all departments.

STEVE: You really are sick in the bonce!

KATYA: There's even a priapic pine cone lodged in my bra. (*Producing the cone.*) Yet another of Nature's tumescent mementoes.

PIP: Mum, for God's sake, pull yourself together.

KATYA: (*Savouring her wine.*) Oh don't be such a little prude, dear.

PIP: I'm not a little prude. It's just very embarrassing having a mother who's a...well, a conifer nympho.

(*KATYA laughs and pours DON and MARK some wine.*)

STEVE: Your mother needs to see a shrink!

KATYA: I've never felt saner in my life.

STEVE: Saner?

KATYA: (*Toasting STEVE.*) And it's all due to you, hubby. And you, Pip. And, of course, we mustn't forget you, Judith.

JUDITH: (*Snatching the bottle from KATYA and pouring herself the rest of the wine.*) Don't blame me for your nymphomaniacal tendencies.

KATYA: I'm not blaming you for anything. Indeed, far from blaming you, Big Jude...

JUDITH: (*Interrupting.*) 'Big Jude'!?

KATYA: (*Relentless.*) ...Instead I want to thank the three of you for freeing me.

PIP: Freeing you from what?

KATYA: Everything. (*Savouring her wine.*) Mmm...isn't this Alsace Sylvaner delicious?

JUDITH: How can we possibly have 'freed' you?

KATYA: Oh come now, Judy-pooh, you know perfectly well if you three... (*Wagging a mocking finger at STEVE, PIP and JUDITH.*) ...hadn't come to my rescue with your little conspiracy...

STEVE: Little conspiracy?

KATYA: Yes, dear, but I do wish you'd stop interrupting me merely to repeat me.

(*During this, KATYA has opened the third bottle and is pouring herself a large one.*)

STEVE: 'S'trewth, she's now going to be pissed as well as nuts.

JUDITH: (*Starting to clear away the picnic things.*) I don't give a monkey's turd what she is. I'm going to do my share of clearing up this culinary travesty, then I'm going to high-tail it outta here. (*To DON.*) Well, don't just sit there drooling over her neck-line, Pop-Eye, give us a hand.

(*KATYA laughs as JUDITH and DON begin to pack the picnic things in the hamper.*)

KATYA: (*To STEVE and PIP.*) Isn't it wonderful to think that I'll never cook or wash up for any of you ever again.

STEVE: Alright, Katya, now you've had your fun, instead of talking round in circles, why don't you come straight out with it and tell me why you're leaving me?

KATYA: Because I'm sick of being as dishonest as you three. (*Indicating JUDITH, STEVE and PIP.*) Mind, until I plucked up the courage to hire that van and pack up all my stuff, *I* was being just as dishonest. If not more so. Day in day out I was literally burying myself under kilos of Russian Classics because they were so romantically morbid. Dostoyevsky, Tolstoy, Turgenev, Gorki, Pushkin, Chekhov, Pasternak, Ostrovsky; you name him and I was under him. I've never lived through so much snow and so many duels in all my life.

STEVE: What's all this Ruski rubbish got to do with why you're leaving me?

KATYA: For eight months I've done nothing but hide behind their characters and be in love with their thoughts. All to avoid facing you three. Talk about exemplary cowardice in the field. My problem was I hadn't the courage to rip open my… (*Trying to laugh.*) …well, my…

PIP: Your what, Mum?

KATYA: (*Staring vacantly at her hand.*) My wound, dear.

JUDITH: Jeez, she's not only tanked-up and raving, she's now got a stigmata complex into the bargain.

KATYA: (*Surging to her feet.*) For Christ sake, Big Jude, give your hypocrisy a miss for once and stop pretending that *I'm* the one who's imagining things. Why don't you admit that the moment you saw me coming out of the wood, you knew that I knew everything.

STEVE: Katya, I swear – on my mother's grave – I don't know what you're burbling on about.

PIP: Granny's still alive, Dad.

STEVE: Alright then, on my father's grave!

KATYA: Okay, if that's the way you want to play it, we'll leave it all unsaid and just get on with our separate lives. (*KATYA wrenches open the cottage door but PIP prevents her from going inside.*)

PIP: Mum, you can't possibly live in there now it's winter. There's no electricity.

KATYA: I'll get by with lots of candles, my Primus stove and the occasional log fire.

DON: How are you going to get the logs?

KATYA: By chopping down the occasional tree, of course.

STEVE: (*Laughing.*) You can't chop down a bleeding tree.

KATYA: Did I neglect to mention that I was the best lumberjack girl-guide in Dorking?

JUDITH: Katya, I really think you should wait at least until next summer to live in this shit hole. That way you won't end up with icicles sticking outta your ass.

KATYA: (*Smiling.*) I've always had a penchant for icicles. Besides, the winter is a genuine challenge. And I need something that's genuine. What's the point of going it alone in the summer? Even old Rousseau managed the summer. But if I can survive an old-fashioned English winter, without acquiring pneumonia, hypothermia and rotting away with loneliness, there is a fair chance that I can survive anything. Now don't sulk, Stephen. Remember, in life, there are no winners. Only long-distance runners. So I'm grateful to you all. But for your conspiracy of silence, I would never have acquired the courage to take myself on like this. By the way, Stephen; I've given up being a five-and-a-half-day-a-week librarian.

STEVE: You can't!

KATYA: (*Cheerfully.*) I know but I have. So I'll only be doing two and a half days a week from now on. I'll have to pull in my belt a notch or two, of course. Still...judicious dieting never hurt anyone, except Tescos.

MARK: You intend to live here by the lake completely by yourself, Mrs Wendover?

KATYA: Certainly. (*Winking.*) I want to get to know all those giant pines even more intimately. Don't worry, my dears. It's just another beginning. For all of us. (*Taking MARK's hand.*) See, I've stopped shaking. I don't even feel panicky anymore. 'Fact I'm almost calm. (*Releasing MARK's hand.*) So now if you'll all excuse me...

MARK: Before you hibernate, Mrs Wendover, can't you at least give us a teensy-weensy clue as to what the dickens is going on?

KATYA: (*Touching his face affectionately.*) You truly don't know, do you?

STEVE: Nor does anyone else!

KATYA: It's hardly worth mentioning really.

DON: Then the least you can do is mention it!

KATYA: (*Adjusting her hat at a rakish angle.*) It's simply that my dear husband and your darling wife have been regularly 'at it', like well-honed knives, since Lady Day last March.

(*DON looks at STEVE and JUDITH's faces. They obviously think that KATYA is crazy.*)

DON: When you say they've been 'at it', you're not suggesting that they've been...

KATYA: (*Smiling.*) ...Making the beast with two backs, yes. He's not only laid her on our lawn, but he's frigged her in our front room, poked her in our pantry and humped her in our henhouse. 'Fact they've probably had wholesale rumpy-pumpy all round the County.

(*STEVE and JUDITH are now laughing and shaking their heads in disbelief.*)

DON: (*Who is also laughing.*) Steve's right, Katya; you need serious psychiatric help.

KATYA: Really?

DON: Yes. You only have to take one look at your husband and my wife to know damn well that he can't have been...frigging her in your front room, poking her in your pantry, humping her in your hen-house and indulging in wholesale rumpy-pumpy all round the County. (*To JUDITH and STEVE.*) Well, how could you? (*Pause.*) You couldn't. Where the hell is your evidence, Katya?

(*Pause.*)

KATYA: (*Indicating JUDITH and STEVE.*) What about their unnatural silence for a start?

DON: Of course they're bloody silent! They're totally dumbfounded. And who can blame 'em? You haven't produced a single piece of evidence to support your sexual paranoia. And that is what you're suffering from, Katya! Well, have you actually seen them even touch one another recently, let alone...?

KATYA: (*Cutting him.*) No. And that's what originally aroused my suspicions.

STEVE: Oh for Chrissakes, Katya, you know that I've never laid a finger on Judy.

KATYA: Not recently. At least not in public. But you and Big Jude used to be very physical with each other.

JUDITH: You can be as screwy as you like, Katya, but you can cut out the 'Big Jude' bit.

KATYA: Well, it's true, Big Jude. In the old days – every time you two met – you always indulged in an exploratory cuddle, followed by several fervid neck nuzzles. Not to mention all the bawdy innuendoes and the statutory goosing. Oh I know it was just good clean Anglo-American fun. But then suddenly, just before Lady Day last year, I noticed that all the fun stopped. Since then you've never cuddled, nuzzled, innuendoed or goosed, or done anything even remotely friendly, in public. But, by Christ, you don't half make up for it in private! Though I only caught you *in flagrante delicto* the once, and that was on Lady Day last year. And the location of your stallion performance, Stephen, was most apposite; being the dungy rear of one of our clapped-out stables. Talk about 'Dick' Turpin's ride to York. Mind, I would have missed viewing the ride had I not had the misfortune to be passing the stables when it started to bucket with rain. Naturally I nipped inside to shelter, where I was just in time to witness the heart-felt whinnying of your thoroughbred mare, Big Jude here. No point in shaking your head, Jude, because after that I began to notice that my randy little steed would often nip over the fence to where the grass was greener, for a quick nibble followed by a prolonged mount, at the oddest times of the day or night.

(*PIP seizes her mother's hand.*)

PIP: Mum, stop it, please!

KATYA: (*Withdrawing her hand.*) But I soon grew used to my bronco's wanderings, because I knew nothing could ever again be as hurtful as that rainy Lady Day afternoon. Although, in truth, Lady Day night was even worse. I couldn't sleep. 'Fact I was so distraught that I pondered whether perhaps I should muffle up in my moth-eaten, imitation mink, then decorously lay my head on the railway line in front of the next holiday special, à la Anna Karenina.

PIP: For pity's sake, Mum, don't go on, I can't bear it!

KATYA: But being only a quarter Russian on my mother's side, and a well-brought-up convent gel to boot, who once flirted with the entire male section of the Hull Polytechnic for a whole term, I soon realised that Tolstoyian suicide wasn't really my style. So I decided – rather than do away with myself – I'd make myself a large glass of Russian tea, complete with three heaped spoonfuls of gooseberry jam. After which, I cried myself to sleep over the gory axe-job in 'Crime and Punishment' to the accompanying strains of 'The Sugar Plum Fairy'. So, all in all, no one can say that I haven't had a very full life. But the crying is over now. The lying is over, too. Henceforward I'm going to be as free as that fucking great swan out there.

(*Pause.*)

DON: (*Laughing and clapping derisively.*) Very droll, Katya, but I don't believe a word of it. 'Fact, after that, I'd be surprised if you have got any friends left at all.
(*Indicating STEVE and JUDITH.*) Well, if I'd've been in their shoes, I'd've upped and left minutes ago.

KATYA: (*Smiling and nodding.*) Exactly.

DON: (*Smiling and nodding.*) How can you go on nodding and grinning when you've just accused my wife and your husband of adultery on an unbelievable scale? Well, I refuse to entertain it. Whatever else my wife is, she is not a…slut. (*Turning to JUDITH.*) Well, don't just sit there, Judith, puffing on your fag. Why don't you deny this slander, for Christ sake? Deny it!

JUDITH: (*After a pause.*) I wish I could, honey, but, God forgive me, I can't.

DON: You mean…?

JUDITH: Yeah; I'm afraid it's all true. (*To KATYA.*) Though I'd no idea that you'd actually…seen us. I'm so very sorry.

KATYA: So was I. At the time.

DON: God in Hell, Steve! I thought you were my best friend.

(*For once STEVE is silent.*)

KATYA: (*To PIP.*) And to make things even nicer, *you've* known all about it for ages, too, haven't you, dear? Yet you never breathed a word.

PIP: (*In tears.*) The reason I didn't tell you when I first guessed what was going on was…well, I didn't want to hurt you, Mummy. Or you, Don. I thought if I kept it to myself…perhaps it would all go away. Oh God, what an awful cockup.

MARK: Literally, by the sounds of it. (*Realising what he has said.*) Oh hell. Sorry.

DON: It's unbelievable. Totally unbelievable.

KATYA: Yes, but I'm sure you will get to believe it in time, my dear. Now I think we'd better call it a day, don't you? The picnic's over. (*To STEVE.*) And you are trespassing on my land.

STEVE: Look, darling, if you'll just let me explain…

KATYA: (*Cutting him.*) Stephen, I'd like to be alone if you don't mind. For a couple of years at least.

(*KATYA goes into the cottage.*)

STEVE: Katya, please give me a chance to explain!

(*The cottage door is heard being locked and bolted from inside.*)

Katya, be reasonable, for God's sake!

DON: Goddam you, Judith. Goddam you both!

(*DON runs off into the trees.*)

JUDITH: Don, please, don't just… (*Running after him.*) Sweetheart, we've got to talk this through. Running away is gonna solve nothing. (*Her voice grows fainter as she runs after him.*) Don! Don honey! Please!

(*MARK gets up to go.*)

PIP: Where are you going?

MARK: To have a chat with your Mum's pine tree. See you around.

PIP: Mark…?

MARK: (*Cutting her.*) Sometime never.

(*MARK goes into the woods.*)

STEVE: Well, get after him, lass. He's a bit on the slow side but he's nice enough – if you have to love a berk in the food trade.

PIP: How could you go on having your disgusting affair with that bitch when you knew bloody well what Mum was going through?

STEVE: Are you any better?

PIP: Me?

STEVE: Yeah. Only reason you didn't tell your Mum about me and Judy was 'cause you wanted a quiet life. You didn't want to face the flak.

PIP: It wasn't my fault that I had to swat up for my 'A' levels all last year, was it?

STEVE: If you hadn't been gadding about with your various boyfriends, you wouldn't've needed to have 'swatted up' because then you'd've passed your 'A' Levels first time round, wouldn't you?

PIP: I got Art first go!

STEVE: Yes, and you should've got English and History as well, and be at some University now, instead of being a receptionist for half dead moggies at that so-called vets you work for.

PIP: You can criticise me all you like, Dad. But the only thing that matters now is what are you going to do about, Mum?

(*STEVE finishes clearing up the picnic.*)

STEVE: It's more a question of what your Mum is going to do about your Mum. Well, one thing's certain. She won't be able to stick it out alone here by the lake. (*Indicating the cottage.*) Not in that shit-pit, she won't.

PIP: (*Helping her father with the clearing up.*) I wouldn't rely on it.

STEVE: She hasn't a chance of holding out. For a kick-off she's scared shitless of the dark. Not to mention being terrified of the local sex-maniac and the county flasher.

And if they don't get her, the snow will. Like it got Napoleon and Hitler. But most of all, there'll be those endless short, grey days and interminable long black nights. On top of which, no one can bear to be alone for very long.

PIP: Hermits can.

STEVE: (*Laughing.*) Your Mum's no ruddy hermit. She's jsut a little convent-cum-grammar school middle-class 'gel' who's a product of the Welfare State and Gold Top milk, so she hasn't got an earthly.

PIP: You're a monster, Dad, you know that? You don't even feel guilty.

STEVE: 'Course I do. We non-conformist sensualists feel little else. But I know your Mum well enough to let things run their own course.

PIP: Rubbish, you don't understand women at all. If you did, you'd go down on your bended knees and beg Mum to come back to you. So stop being such a turd face and plead with her to come home with us.

STEVE: And miss all the fun? (*In broad Lancashire.*) Nay, lass. Be too easy, an' Life's supposed to be 'ard. (*Grinning.*) Otherwise it wouldn't be Life, would it? (*Chuckling, STEVE goes off into the trees, carrying various chairs and bags. As he disappears, he calls over his shoulder.*) When you've finished clearing up, bring the remnants of the Last Supper home with you, there's a good little disciple. We're going to need every scrap of grub we can lay our mitts on. (*PIP slams the rest of things into carrier bags. Then she bangs on the cottage door.*)

PIP: (*Shouting.*) Mum, you can't leave us like this! It's not right! Dad'll never manage on his own. He's a totally useless, selfish prat. Nor will you! That's why you're married to each other. (*Banging harder.*) Mum, for pity's sake, be reasonable. (*The bedroom window opens and KATYA pokes her head out.*)

KATYA: Only one pint, please, milkman. And not Gold Top, if you don't mind.

PIP: Mum, this is no time for your stupid games.

KATYA: And six eggs, a pound of rindless streaky, half of unsalted butter, and Napoleon's pine tree in a snow storm with the local sex-maniac with nobs.

PIP: How can you be so frivolous when everything's in ruins?

KATYA: Don't be such a glum-chops, dear. The world doesn't end till New Year's Eve. Besides, I think it's all been rather a giggle. Especially your poor father. I've never seen so much badly-disguised desperation and non-conformist panic. But don't worry, Pipa, I'm going to have the time of my life. Indeed I wouldn't be surprised if I didn't have the time of all our lives.
(*Still laughing, KATYA closes the window, leaving PIP stunned.*
The blackbird starts singing in the woods.
Distraught, PIP collects the remainder of the picnic things.
Then, weighed down with them and her own unhappiness,
PIP trudges out of sight.
The blackbird's song is jubilant as it starts to snow.)

Scene 2

Same setting, but with several additions, including three large logs (positioned as seats) overlooking the lake. There is a table under the cottage window, and an axe in a pile of wood near the apple tree.

17 January. Six weeks later. Just before dusk.

Occasional snow flakes drift down but fail to settle on the black frost that grips the woods.

KATYA appears from behind the apple tree. She is wearing an old coat, paint-stained jeans and heavy boots. Abruptly she stops and crouches among the tree roots. She examines the bark of the tree. She seems immune to the cold.

KATYA: Miraculous.
(*MARK, now without his spectacles, emerges from behind the cottage. He is wearing a smart overcoat, silk scarf and kid gloves.*)

MARK: What's miraculous?

KATYA: (*Without looking at him.*) Stop spying on me, Mark. It's becoming remarkably tedious.

MARK: (*Grinning.*) Only taking a leaf out of your book, Mrs Wendover.

KATYA: At least I did mine from a distance, via binoculars and lip-reading.

MARK: Sorry but I can't get over you.

KATYA: Am I supposed to take that metaphorically or literally?

MARK: Didn't mean I was trying to 'get over you' like that. Though I wish I could.

KATYA: Mark! That's not like you at all.

MARK: (*Grinning.*) I know. Isn't it great? What's more, since we last met, I've even read a couple of books from cover to cover.

KATYA: Congratulations.

MARK: King Arthur and the Round Table's my favourite. 'Specially like the sexy bits with Queen Guinevere and Lancelot.

KATYA: Oh dear.

MARK: (*Subsiding on a log.*) D'you realise it's six weeks since your cock-up of a picnic? (*Quickly.*) ...I mean, since you decided to hibernate down here.

KATYA: Seems centuries.

MARK: It's unnatural for humans to hibernate.

KATYA: Maybe I'm not human any more. My ears have definitely got furrier. Not to mention acquiring my tail.

MARK: Right little tease, aren't you?

KATYA: Hardly surprising considering the tutors I've had.

MARK: You mean your randy hubby and Mrs K?

KATYA: No, I mean the squirrels, insects – and this Puss Moth pupa.

MARK: Puss what?

KATYA: Puss Moth pupa. Don't touch the bark! The pupa's hibernating in the crevice. There – see.

MARK: And that's a Puss Moth pupa?

KATYA: Yes, and the sleeping caterpillar inside that yellow ball of fluff is alive and well and living in England.

Which is more than can be said for most of my
contemporaries. This summer the caterpillar's body will
chemically break down and reform into the body of a
Puss Moth. Then the pupa will split. The moth will crawl
out, dry its damp wings and whirr off into the dusk.
That's what I call miraculous. Hey, watch where you're
galumphing your hobnail boots. There's a couple of
cardinal beetles kipping down there.

MARK: Jesus, you're right.

KATYA: They're like medieval warriors in their crimson
armour, aren't they?

MARK: Wouldn't go that far.

KATYA: Oh come now, have you ever seen anything as
gorgeous as these two little cardinals?

MARK: Yes; you!

KATYA: There's nothing more flattering than being
compared to a beetle.

MARK: But you are gorgeous. It's only the way you're
living that's grotesque.

KATYA: Charmed, I'm sure.

MARK: Not that I don't envy you, I do. 'Fact it's mainly
because of you that I've made a momentous decision
today.

KATYA: (*Wielding the axe to chop some wood.*) Shouldn't you
be back at your supermarket by now?

MARK: (*Shaking his head.*) *That* was my momentous
decision. This afternoon I told my boss where he could
stuff my job.

KATYA: Why?

MARK: I've decided I'm not cut out to work in
supermarkets. I've got bigger fish to fry. That's why I
resigned this lunch time so I could come down here and
live with you!
(*KATYA is so shaken by this that she nearly chops her own
foot off.*)

KATYA: Now wait one minute, Mark!

MARK: I'll wait all night if necessary. Just so long as you
let me move in with you.

(*MARK tries to embrace KATYA but she backs away from him, stumbling over a log but still holding her axe.*)

KATYA: (*Waving an admonishing finger.*) Now stop being a silly-billy, Mark.

MARK: Is it silly to fall madly in love with a wildly sensual, passionate creature like you?

(*MARK takes the axe from her.*)

KATYA: What d'you think you're doing?

MARK: (*Throwing the axe on the wood pile.*) Ever since that amazing picnic, I've not been able to think of anything else but you stuck down here all alone, dancing naked in the frost.

KATYA: I don't dance naked in the frost.

MARK: Alright then; half-naked. Like you were on that glorious December afternoon, showing off all your wondrous wares. Let's face it, you're the biggest turn-on since sliced bread!

KATYA: (*Laughing.*) I suppose that's a compliment of sorts.

(*MARK grabs her and kisses her. She half responds, then gently extricates herself.*)

My goodness me, you do have such erotic eyelashes.

MARK: You wait till you see the rest of me!

KATYA: (*Backing away.*) I'm sure.

MARK: D'you mind if I kiss you again? You taste unbelievably yummy.

(*KATYA picks up the axe to ward him off.*)

KATYA: This is completely absurd.

MARK: Yeah, but isn't it 'miraculous'?

(*KATYA goes on with her chopping. MARK tries to restrain her.*)

KATYA: Mark, let go of me and be a good boy.

MARK: You've no idea how often I've lain on my bed and dreamt of slowly taking your clothes off. Well, ripping 'em off, actually.

(*Still wrestling for possession of the axe, MARK pulls KATYA towards him in an attempt to kiss her. KATYA lets go of the axe and beats a hasty retreat round the tree.*)

Katya!

KATYA: (*Peering at him from the safety of the tree.*) Can you really see me without your glasses?

MARK: You are a bit of a blur. (*Discarding the axe and sidling towards her.*) But I thought you might find me more sexy without them.

(*Again MARK tries to kiss her but at the last moment KATYA moves her head, and MARK ends up with a mouthful of bark.*)

Buggerwugger! (*Whipping his spectacles out of his pocket.*) Look, we can make love with my glasses on if you like. If it's the professorial approach turns you on.

KATYA: You really are quite cute. In an impossible sort of way.

MARK: You've got such lovely hair. And superb breasts.

KATYA: (*Laughing but flattered.*) Oh do you really think so?

MARK: Absolutely. As for your bottom – well, the hours it's given me a lift in Tesco's warehouse is nobody's business. So why don't we go in and celebrate the fact that – as a piece of womanhood – you're the sexiest going?

(*KATYA laughs as MARK pulls her into his arms and kisses her. Despite herself she responds, then she breaks away.*)

KATYA: Impossible.

MARK: Why?

KATYA: I'm not saying there isn't part of me that wouldn't like to 'celebrate' – but unfortunately I can't.

MARK: Why not?

KATYA: (*Smiling.*) I've taken this vow of Everlasting Chastity.

MARK: Everlasting?!

KATYA: Well...at least until Easter.

MARK: When did you make this stupid vow?

KATYA: (*Retrieving the axe.*) This morning. Over my Shreddies.

MARK: You're taking the piss again, aren't you?

KATYA: (*Starting chopping.*) On the contrary. My Chastity Vow was my prime contribution to Candlemas.

MARK: Candlemas?

KATYA: The Feast of the Purification of the Virgin Mary. Though the Christian interpretation of the Feast was not established until the Fifth Century, when it replaced the Roman Festival of the Goddess Febura, in whose honour thousands of vestal virgins carried glowing candles through the streets of Ancient Rome.

MARK: Now hang on, you said...

KATYA: (*Overriding him.*) ...But the purification rites were observed not only by the vestal virgins, but by all the women.

MARK: Yes, but you just said that the women did that virgin bit in honour of the Roman Goddess February...Febura.

KATYA: They did.

MARK: But today is only the seventeenth of bleeding January!

KATYA: Ah...well...although it's true that the actual Feast of Candlemas doesn't take place officially until the Second of February, I always like to celebrate these Holy Days a fortnight early.

MARK: (*Watching KATYA pile logs into a barrow.*) Why the hell d'you want to celebrate it a fortnight early?

KATYA: To get in practice, of course. Besides, there's a full moon tonight. That alone is worth celebrating.

MARK: I don't see what a full moon's got to do with a two-week-early Candlemas?

KATYA: Believe me, when you live alone through a grim winter, you soon appreciate why our ancestors practised the ancient rituals of fire and re-birth from Yuletide to Easter. Especially on evenings such as this; when the sunset is like a weeping wound, and the moon is so monstrously white, it seems as if it's about to devour the sky.

MARK: (*Laughing.*) You're trying to spook me out, aren't you?

KATYA: One thing is certain, if our ancestors in the Dark Ages hadn't had festivals and feast days to look forward

to during the long winters, they'd have certainly
'spooked' themselves right out of their wits. Remember,
they had no telly, pop songs or the Internet to
anaesthetise them against the long nights and the cold.
So the villagers in the Dark Ages held onto their rituals,
to keep them in touch with their dead parents and
children. But there was nothing morbid about it. The
rituals gave them a reassuring sense of continuity. And
they needed that continuity because the Early Church
insisted that the villagers knelt down and kissed the
Virgin Mary's sky-blue, Persil Automatic-washed skirts –
even though most of them didn't believe in the Virgin,
because they secretly worshipped the Triple Moon
Goddess, who was the source of Nature's annual fertility.
The villagers knew that without a good harvest, they
would starve to death next winter. So come Candlemas,
the elders illumined the darkness with fiery will-o'-the-
wisps in the snow. They chanted invocations to the gaunt
trees as they solemnly danced in homage to the full
moon, with the wind keening in the branches and the
owls as hooded sentinels. And what was good enough for
our ancestors, Mark, is more than good enough for me.
Oh I know you probably regard this – to quote my ex-
husband – (*In a Northern accent.*) – 'as yet another
example of her pissin' feyness'. But I don't care because I
believe there are a lot of people who still secretly agree
with me. They also want to keep in touch with their past,
and have a love affair with clean air, and green woods
and unpolluted lakes. Trouble is, most of us are too
scared to commit ourselves to what we believe in. We're
embarrassed by what other people might think of us. So
what do we do? We shrink back into ourselves because
we're too bloody chicken to admit that we, too, crave to
be an integral part of the earth's fecund rhythms!

MARK: I'm not too chicken to admit that I crave to be an
integral part of *your* fecund rhythms.

KATYA: (*Laughing.*) Sorry, Mark, but this is the first
Chastity Vow I've ever made. What's more, I fully intend
to keep it. At least until it's properly dark.

(*KATYA wheels the barrow to the lean-to beside the cottage.*)

MARK: (*Following her.*) You mean, once it's dark we can start bonking.

KATYA: Well...it's possible.

MARK: That's in about five minutes' time. WHOOPEE!

KATYA: Doesn't it worry you that we'll be betraying my daughter?

MARK: Did it worry Pipa when she betrayed you?

(*Again MARK tries to embrace KATYA but she foils him.*)

KATYA: I do wish you wouldn't keep chasing me round this tree!

MARK: (*Continuing to chase her.*) I can't help myself, baby, I want you so badly.

KATYA: (*Fending him off with the wheelbarrow.*) But there's no way I can possibly live up to your carnal expectations. 'Fact I doubt whether even Cleopatra could.

MARK: (*Jumping over the wheelbarrow to embrace her.*) Don't worry, my little Serpent of the Nile; you're going to be sextraordinary!

KATYA: Oh dear, I do believe I'm about to panic.

MARK: A wildly sensual, passionate creature like you never panics.

KATYA: No, but a Gold Top, convent-cum-grammar-school gel certainly does.

MARK: Oh for God's sake, let's stop fighting and go in and start bonking. (*Lunging at her.*) Well, look – it's nearly dark now.

KATYA: (*Warding him off.*) Alright, alright.

MARK: You will?!

KATYA: On one condition.

MARK: Name it and I'll sign it.

KATYA: You must promise me that once we've done the deed of darkness that you'll go straight back to your job. Then you'll stop being a randy roaringboy pillock and marry my daughter and leave me in peace.

MARK: Oh Katya!

KATYA: (*Overriding him.*) Promise!

MARK: Can't we do first things first?

KATYA: PROMISE!

MARK: (*After a pause.*) Okay. If it turns out like you think it's going to turn out; i.e., the biggest sexual disaster of the century; then I promise you'll never see hide nor hair of me again. But if it turns out – as I'm sure it will be – to be fan-fucking-tastic, then you've got to let me stay on here with you to fight off all my rivals. Agreed?
(*MARK opens the cottage door and beckons.*)

KATYA: (*Joining him in the doorway.*) Oh alright. Now come in and close the door before I change my mind.
(*KATYA disappears inside the cottage.*)

MARK: (*Still in the doorway.*) You kip down here in the front parlour, do you? How convenient.
(*MARK goes inside. The door closes on KATYA's laughter.*
It is now night. The moon has risen, making the cottage and the frosty woods seem unnaturally luminous. Ducks quack inanely on the lake.
There is a strange, snuffling sound from the woods. Someone is moving stealthily through the dead leaves.
Moments later, a figure crawls out of the trees, cowled in an old coat. Cautiously the figure slithers towards the cottage, then pauses to swig some milk from a bottle. The prolonged belch that follows reveals DON's disgruntled identity. DON throws back his coat hood, takes another swig, then crawls forward again.
In the distance, he hears the sound of hounds baying. He freezes. The baying dies away. He crawls forward again.
KATYA's silhouette appears in the cottage window. DON ducks behind the wood pile. KATYA can now be seen in the window, lighting a candle. Then she retreats into the darkness of the parlour.
Commando-style, DON edges forward until he is under the window. Then DON levers himself to his feet and peers into the candlelit room.)

DON: (*Roaring in fury at what he sees inside the cottage.*) Joseph Bleeding Stalin!
(*DON pulls a torch out of his pocket, wrenches open the cottage door and shines the torch on the occupants inside.*)
You lecherous, four-eyed, little bonker!

KATYA: (*Inside; very cool.*) How dare you come barging in here, Donald, and address my guest in that peremptory manner?

DON: I might equally ask what your guest's doing halfway out of his Marks and Spencer Y-Fronts?

(*DON charges into the cottage. His torch beam flashes across the window.*)

KATYA: (*Still inside.*) We were about to have a *bijou tête-à-tête.*

DON: (*Inside.*) More like 'tit-à-tit'!

(*MARK comes rushing out of the cottage in his unbuttoned shirt and Y-Fronts.*)

MARK: (*Calling over his shoulder.*) Gimme my trousers back, you big bully!

(*DON appears, holding MARK's trousers.*)

DON: You'll need more than these pants to save you from what I've got in mind.

(*DON advances on MARK, who backs away, protecting his genitalia.*)

MARK: Typical. Whenever a politician's outflanked, he immediately resorts to violence.

DON: Watch your mouth, you Waitrose wanker!

MARK: I don't work for wanking Waitrose, I work for tossing Tescos!

(*KATYA appears in the doorway, fighting her way into her jeans.*)

KATYA: Yes, Donald, that's quite enough of what passes as Parliamentary wit for one evening. Now give Mark his trousers back.

DON: No way. I enjoy watching him dancing round the woods in his undies.

KATYA: So do I. But for other reasons. Now stop being envious and give him back his pants.

(*KATYA disappears into the cottage. DON is about to chase MARK when KATYA's head re-appears around the door.*)

Hand them over this instant, Donald, or I shall never speak to you again.

DON: Alright, alright.

(*DON throws the trousers into MARK's face. KATYA goes back into the cottage. Shivering, MARK puts on his pants.*)

MARK: 'Cause of you, I've got goose bumps in the most highly sensitive of places.

(*DON laughs and sits on the trestle table under the window. KATYA re-appears with MARK's jacket, overcoat and shoes.*)

KATYA: Unfortunately it has turned out to be a Dionisiac debacle.

MARK: (*Taking his glasses out of his trouser pockets and putting his glasses on.*) Oh don't worry, sweetheart, I'm still coming back to try again tomorrow.

DON: Oh no you're not, Bifocals.

KATYA: (*Affectionately ruffling MARK's hair.*) Yes, it really is pointless, dear.

MARK: Why?

KATYA: I believe in living each moment to the hilt, as it were; but unfortunately you didn't even manage to get yours out of its scabbard.

MARK: (*Fighting his way into his trousers.*) I'm still coming back tomorrow.

DON: If I as much glimpse your greengrocer's goggles ever again, I'll snap your cucumber over my knee.

MARK: (*Tugging on his socks.*) Take a better man than you, Gunga Din. 'Cause I'm still going to have her in the end, 'cause I'm in love with her.

DON: You don't know what love means, boy.

KATYA: Do you, Donald?

DON: Yes, I do, God damn and blast it!

KATYA: (*Stepping between the two men.*) Donald, I'd like a word with Mark alone, if you don't mind.

DON: I do mind!

KATYA: Donald!

DON: Alright, alright, I'll let you have a word with him. (*Indicating the cottage.*) But you're certainly not going to have it in there.

KATYA: (*Taking MARK's arm.*) Then let's sample the woods, dear.

DON: (*Shining the torch in MARK's face.*) I meant everything I said, boyo.

MARK: So did I – Senior Citizen.

(*KATYA and MARK walk into the woods, illuminated by DON's torch. Just before they disappear, MARK turns round and gives DON the V sign.*

DON is about to attack MARK when there is a sudden loud splash in the lake. DON whirls round, shining his torch over the water – into the audience's eyes. There is another splash, even louder.

DON moves down to the bulrushes and peers over the moonlit lake; the ripples reflecting on his face. Ducks quack in the distance. There is a sudden whirr of wings as two swans fly off into the night.

DON shines his torch into the night sky, watching the swans fly over head.)

DON: I certainly wouldn't mind being a swan tonight.

(*The sound of the swans' wings die away. There are two distinct splashes in the lake. Mystified, DON crouches in the reeds and peers over the water.*

KATYA re-appears from the wood. She is alone. She sees that DON is spellbound, so she tries to sneak unnoticed back to the cottage.

DON shines the torch in KATYA's face as she reaches the cottage steps.)

Who made that great hole in the ice?

KATYA: I did.

DON: We've become a real backwood's girl, haven't we?

(*KATYA joins him by the lake.*)

KATYA: No, but the ice on a lake is like an iron cowl on a live child. It's murderous to wildlife. Birds starve to death. Fish expire for lack of oxygen. The least I could do was hack a hole in the middle of the lake and give them a chance to breathe.

DON: You really have changed, haven't you?

KATYA: Have I?

(*There is another loud splash in the lake.*)

DON: What the hell's that?

KATYA: A pike. Hunting.

DON: Katya, there's something I have to discuss with you.

KATYA: Three nights ago, before the lake froze over, there were two enormous pike having a fight to the death under those lily pads.

DON: Katya, it's very important...

KATYA: (*Overriding him.*) The larger of the two pike rammed its grey snout down the other's fanged gullet. I've never seen such ferocity. It made my hair stand on end.

DON: You sure you didn't imagine it?

KATYA: Under a full moon, you can't be sure of anything. (*Staring into the night sky.*) Especially when the sky is aching with stars, like tonight. The effect on me is always the same. Whenever I look up on a frosty evening and see trillions upon trillions of pulsing lights, my entire stability is blown away. You see, I know that most of those pin-pricks of fire are as big as our footling little earth, if not bigger. So who the hell is Katya Wendover compared to all that? All those stars make me feel that I'm just a bra-and-pantied microbe who's poncing about on an extinct mammoth's conk.
(*DON laughs.*)
Well, it's true; I'm not even significant enough to make this hairy old mammoth of a universe itch. Let alone get it to sneeze. So what significance do we have to anything? – in the face of all those twinkling pterodactyls up there.

DON: Now don't tell me you do nothing but mooch around this lake every night agonising about the firmament?

KATYA: 'Course not! But I do occasionally enjoy asking myself questions that no one can answer. Makes me feel almost intellectual. And I like that. Once a quarter.

DON: So I gather. By the way, in the Great Pike Battle, which monster won?

KATYA: Neither. The two pike tore each other to shreds. But there's nothing new in that. We do it all the time. Anyway, you're trespassing, Donald. So for both our sakes, you'd best vamoose.

DON: You've fallen in love with that goggle-eyed little prick, haven't you?

KATYA: It's not so little. Besides, I find his frenetic innocence refreshing. There's not much of it about these days. God knows, I wish I still had some of it. (*Turning back to the cottage.*) But perhaps I never did.

DON: (*Barring her way.*) You're incredibly unhappy, aren't you?

KATYA: (*Laughing and shaking her head.*) On the contrary, I've never felt so elated in all my life. 'Fact I'm 'so excited', I scarcely know how to contain myself.

DON: What's there to be so excited about?

KATYA: This lake, these woods, the frost, the infinity of stars. The deer who sneak up to my window when they think I'm asleep. The weasel in the woodshed, owls in the barn. Then there's the teeming insect life waiting to erupt out of the dead leaves. God in Heaven, if all this didn't excite me, I might as well be...

DON: (*Mischievously.*) ...A bra-and-pantied microbe poncing about on an extinct mammoth's conk?

KATYA: *Touché*, monsieur. The paradoxes are endless. (*Stroking a branch of the apple tree.*) Still...at least the trees and the lake give me the illusion that my childhood innocence can be regained somehow. And if, for one electric moment, I can regain some of that innocence, it would be worth all the effort in the world, surely?

DON: (*Cynical.*) You mean like Milton and his unreadable 'Paradise Regained'?

KATYA: (*Laughing.*) Oh I'm not that far gone. (*Impulsively KATYA kisses DON on the cheek but she breaks away from him as he responds.*) Sleep well, Don. Try not to have too many hurtful dreams. (*KATYA moves to the cottage but DON runs ahead of her and prevents her from entering.*)

DON: It's imperative we go inside and talk.

KATYA: No.

DON: You were quick enough to let Young Goggle-Snout into your inner sanctum!

KATYA: I panicked. Oh I'm not saying it wasn't a delicious sensation but it was pure panic.

(*DON grabs KATYA by the shoulders and kisses her voraciously. After a brief struggle, KATYA fights her way out of his arms.*)

KATYA: Don, what the devil d'you think you're doing?

DON: Trying to make you panic, of course. Well, if you can have an erogenous freak-out with Four-Eyes, you can certainly have one with me.

KATYA: (*Laughing.*) An erogenous freak-out?

DON: Yes. It apparently happens to a lot of women just before they go through the Change. They get ruttish and concupiscent.

KATYA: Whatever's come over you? You're not behaving at all like my favourite up-tight little Puritan with Cromwell in his jockstrap.

DON: (*Waving his arms wildly.*) You don't have to tell me! It happens to men, too, you know.

KATYA: What does?

DON: The Change of bleeding Life! We don't change physically, of course. But we do mentally froth and go screwy. You've no idea how tumescently tizzed-up we faithful blokes get. After forty, they say a man thinks about sex every six and a half minutes. And that's only when he's awake. And I'm talking about men like me, who have always been habitually faithful to their wives. It's suddenly as if my whole adult life has screeched by me, and I've nothing to show for it but a severely dented libido. Well, let's face it, there's been one woman to whom I've given my all – and she's turned out to be Brooklyn's answer to Salome, Jezebel and Mae West rolled into one. (*Slumping down on the bench under the window.*) So all I'm left with now are memories of cramped adolescence, political failure, wasted sperm, a nagging ulcer and ten very raw cuticles.

KATYA: (*Putting a comforting hand on his shoulder.*) Oh come on, it can't be that bad.

DON: It's worse than bad, it's horrendous. (*Indicating the cottage.*) And to compound my misery, from the moment you closeted yourself in the cottage, I've been without a home.

KATYA: What?

DON: There was no way I was going to stay under the same
roof as that adulterous cow. So I went straight up to
London and dossed down in the YMCA. And I've been
there ever since.

KATYA: You haven't!

DON: (*Nodding.*) 'Cept, of course, at weekends, when I've
been down here, patrolling these woods, and watching
the Tesco Tosser, who's been watching you, watching the
herons, watching all those fucking fish fornicate!

KATYA: (*Laughing sympathetically.*) Oh Don.

DON: I just can't see enough of you. I want to be with you
all the time. I can't help it. Well, let's face it, we have got
everything in common.

KATYA: Such as?

DON: We're both rotting away with loneliness and going
quietly batty, not to mention being consumed with
decades of unrequited lust.

KATYA: Speak for yourself.

DON: I am! But most important of all, we both share the
same overwhelming need for love, companionship and
total trust. That's why I've decided to marry you
tomorrow at dawn.

KATYA: You've decided to marry me?!

DON: (*Taking her hand to lead her to the cottage.*) Yes. So let's
go and celebrate before imminent frost-bite nips off all
our festive appendages.

KATYA: (*Breaking away.*) I can't marry you. I'm already
married.

DON: Snap! But that doesn't preclude our having a
pantheist-type nuptial, though, does it?

KATYA: Pantheist?

DON: Yes, we could hold the marriage ceremony in the
bulrushes, with a heron as priest, a coot as best man and
those grey tits as witnesses.

KATYA: You really have gone loop-the-loop, haven't you?

DON: If you don't fancy being married by the fowl of the
air, there's always Reverend Fox to perform the
ceremony, and Mr Badger as best man, with barn owls as

bridesmaids and raunchy rabbits as witnesses. Well, bunnies are professional bigamists.

KATYA: You're as mad as the March Hare.

DON: (*Clasping his hand to her bosom.*) Then you will marry me?

KATYA: Of course not. Now stop being a dumb bunny and lollop home.

(*DON grabs KATYA and pulls her down onto the ground, kissing her hungrily. KATYA tries to extricate herself.*)

Now, Donald, cut that out. You're being immature and unnecessarily crass.

DON: Oooh, there's nothing sexier than a patronising woman.

(*DON pins her down and forcibly kisses her again. KATYA comes up for air, fighting for breath.*)

KATYA: If you do that again, you bastard, I'll knee you in the groin.

DON: (*Pinning her down again.*) Promises, promises.

KATYA: Get off me! My shoulder's gone numb and the grass is freezing my bum.

DON: This is how it used to be with Judith and me in our courting days.

KATYA: (*Still vainly struggling.*) Then I can more than understand why she's started opening her legs elsewhere.

(*DON is about to kiss KATYA again when he is transfixed by a dazzling torch beam.*)

FIGURE: (*Approaching with the torch.*) Glad to see that I'm not the only one who indulges in poking in the pantry, humping in the hen house and wholesale rumpy-pumpy all round the county.

DON: Oh, that...you, Steve?

STEVE: Certainly isn't the Queen of the May. Well, don't just lie there, you poxy git. Get off my wife.

KATYA: (*Snuggling up to DON.*) No, you stay right where you are, Don darling. You're just beginning to warm me up.

STEVE: If he doesn't get off you smartish, I'll kick him in the goolies.

DON: (*Stroking KATYA's hair.*) Sweetheart, how could you have possibly married such a foul-mouthed bourgeois lefty?

STEVE: Nothing fucking foul-mouthed about me, shit-for-brains! Now unthigh my wife this instant, you limp dick. (*KATYA hooks her ankles over DON's.*)

KATYA: 'Fraid he can't, dear. I've pinned him in.

STEVE: You wanton hussy!

KATYA: It's what's known, Stephen, as – 'even Stephens'.

DON: (*Suddenly leaping to his feet.*) Yes, Katya, and 'even Stephens' means that you're going to get even more 'even' with Stephen when you divorce the philandering toss-pot and marry me, right?!

KATYA: (*Getting up.*) No, unfortunately that was just a very bad pun, Donald. Now if you'll both stop loitering with intent and slope off home, I'll get on with the rest of my life.

STEVE: I'm not going anywhere 'till you tell me where you've hidden it.

KATYA: Hidden what?

STEVE: Don't play funny buggers with me, Katya. Driving yourself nuts in these woods is one thing, but stealing my shotgun is quite another.

KATYA: Your shotgun?

STEVE: Yes, so go and fetch it, there's a good little nutter.

KATYA: How can I fetch what I haven't got?

STEVE: Listen, sweetheart, I know how hysterical, lonely and tormented you must be without me at your side, but…

KATYA: (*Interrupting.*) Lonely and tormented? (*Laughing.*) You must be joking.

STEVE: (*Oblivious.*) Yes, and you're so appallingly defenceless and vulnerable.

DON: God save us.

STEVE: Shut it, Kant, will you? (*To KATYA.*) 'Fact I've only just come round to fully appreciating how desperately you must ache for my marauding builder's hands on your lonely librarian's body.

DON: You supercilious sphincter!

STEVE: Look, why don't you just canter off, Kant? It's tricky enough trying to be intimate with one's estranged wife without having one's local ex-MP shouting the odds all the time.

KATYA: Why don't you piss off home, Stephen? I'm sick to the gills with listening to your testosterone twaddle.

STEVE: (*Putting his arm round KATYA's shoulder.*) Oh don't worry, luv, any shrink'll tell you that a frustrated middle-aged woman – and every middle-aged woman *is* frustrated...

KATYA: (*Interrupting as she disengages herself.*) I am not middle-aged! Or frustrated!

STEVE: ...Tends to act extremely irrationally come the full moon. 'Specially if she has a perverse predilection for hibernation, Emily Dickinson and fir-tree-nymphomania.

KATYA: Extraordinary how everyone who's trespassed on my estate tonight is suffering from lunar lunacy, isn't it?

STEVE: Oh I'm not saying that you don't have cause for a feverish freak out. Well, the thought of your athletic husband being in the arms of that Transatlantic sexual-assault course, Big Jude – no offence, Don – is more than enough to shatter any girl's ego. But it's still no reason to steal my shotgun in order to blow your pretty little brains out.

KATYA: Donald dear, will you do me a favour?

DON: Anything.

KATYA: Take Tom O'Bedlam home, then thoroughly sedate him.

STEVE: I see; going to do yourself in with pills now, are you? Mind, they're not as messy as a shotgun.

KATYA: I'm not going 'to do myself in' at all, you primordial sexist.

STEVE: (*Smiling.*) Note the suicidal hysteria in her voice, Don. Sure sign. Still, that's typical of all middle-class, ex-convent-grammar-school dollies. They can't help screeching out the opposite of what they really mean.

(*In disbelief, KATYA slumps down at the table by the window.*)

She's probably in the run up to her period. Always the same. You forget to bring her flowers for some anniversary, then you happen to come home a bit pissed; and there's the little lady, all whey-faced and tear-stained. So you say to her in your best slurred tones... (*Imitating himself when drunk.*) 'Ish there anything wrong, schweetie-pie?' Then, quick as a flash, she shrieks at the top of her vocals: 'No, of course there bloody isn't, you drunken dickhead!' And instantly you know that *everything* is bloody wrong. Trouble is, most blokes are such insensitive slobs they don't realise that all the poor dear really wants is a little masculine attention. But thank Heavens, I'm one of the sensitive few.

KATYA: You, sensitive? What a fully-paid-up arsehole.

STEVE: Oh come on, be fair, sweetheart. If I wasn't sensitive, I wouldn't've packed Judith in once'n for all, would I? What's more, I did it straight after the picnic. That's why I decided to come down here now so I can live with you on a permanent basis.

KATYA: (*Laughing.*) You've decided to come back and live with me?

STEVE: Right. But if it'll help your hurt pride, for public consumption, we can announce that you decided to live with me. What are you guffawing at, Kant?

DON: (*Still laughing in disbelief.*) I thought I was a major male chauvinist porker but you take the Norman Mailer Award.

STEVE: For Chrissakes, go and jump in the lake, Kant, while I finish reasoning with my wife.

DON: (*Bowing ironically.*) Okay, Stevo. Have your brief, little frosty heart-to-heart with the love of my life. When you've finished, I'll come back and collect my bride. (*DON goes off into the wood. KATYA laughs.*)

STEVE: What's the big joke?

KATYA: I never realised madness was so catching.

STEVE: Look, darling, can't you see that I'm, well...I'm doing my damnedest to tell you that I've...well, I've fallen in love with you. Again!

KATYA: It's too late, Stephen. And you know it.

STEVE: Why?

KATYA: Because I now realise that for the last twenty years I must have lobotomised myself, or I would never have been crazy enough to put up with your barbarous builder's ego trip and boorish manners. But now let me tell you, Stephen, I have belatedly come to my senses because enough is more than enough!

STEVE: Now don't start all that crap again, sweetheart.

KATYA: (*Walking away from him.*) My life has been unthinkable. From the moment you first savoured the virginal fruits of my nineteen-year-old body at the rear of the Hull Polytechnic, you have been ladling out that 'crap' – as you so appositely call it – by the trailer load.

STEVE: (*Going to her.*) Katya...

KATYA: (*Keeping him at a distance.*) And the only reason I've continued to stomach your bigoted ranting is because I stupidly believed that it was my duty, as your adoring wife, to suffer habitual middle-class guilt for all those poverty-stricken indignities that you constantly informed me that *you* suffered as a deprived coalminer's son. Mind, we southerners have always proved to be absurdly masochistic whenever there's any guilt-ridden angst in the offing.

(*KATYA snaps an icicle from the window ledge and sucks it like a lollipop.*)

Which is presumably why I like sucking ice. Nothing like an icicle for setting your teeth on edge.

STEVE: Katya, can't you be serious for once, instead of wittering on about masochism and icicles?

KATYA: Oh I'm not saying that it's entirely your fault that our marriage is as dead as the moon. When we were first married, I must admit I found your northern bluntness, bad language and brick-laying approach to love-making rather appealing. So, in a way, without realising it, I encouraged you to become even worse. But unfortunately, Stephen, ever since I witnessed your 'stallion' performance on Lady Day, something inside me has...crumbled. It made me feel like a slice of old wedding cake left out too long in the rain. And it wasn't

only because of my hurt pride. Or jealousy. Or even
because I'd fallen out of love with you. No, it was
something more fundamental. Evening after evening I
came down here by the lake in the early spring, trying to
drown the nightmare of our marriage. The water seemed
to lap around me, cold and implacable. The lake was
totally immune to my distress. It gave me no false
comfort, thank God. Nevertheless over the weeks, I
gradually became aware that I was totally exhausted.
And now I haven't the fortitude to play your indulgent
house-keeping, full-time Mummy anymore.

STEVE: You saying that you've done nothing but 'mother'
me all these years?

KATYA: Of course. (*Cod Northern accent.*) 'Well, ent that
what a lad o' good minin' stock expects o' 'is lass?' Then
at our little picnic I discovered, to my relief, that I'd
outgrown you. I've certainly outgrown *us*. Now don't
glower at me with those hurt eyes. That makes me want
to panic again. Then Heaven knows what I might do out
of pity.

STEVE: I don't want your pity, woman. I want your love
back! But I suppose that's too much to ask, isn't it?

KATYA: Absolutely.

STEVE: How can you be so bloody frigid?

(*DON appears behind STEVE, grinning.*)

DON: Hopping about in the frost can't have helped.

STEVE: I thought I told you to go and jump in the frigging
lake!

DON: I did, but I bounced off the ice.

(*KATYA laughs. DON opens the cottage door for KATYA.*)
Shall we, darling?

STEVE: Hands off her, Kant. She belongs to me!

DON: (*Shaking his head.*) She belongs to me.

(*MARK materialises out of the wood.*)

MARK: Sorry, guys, if she belongs to anyone; it's me.

STEVE: She's mine, I tell you.

DON: By dawn, she'll be mine.

MARK: No, she's mine!

STEVE: No, mine!

THE TRIO: (*In unison.*) Mine, mine, MINE!
   (*Their shouting is suddenly drowned by KATYA who screams as she beats her fists on the table.*)
DON: Now see what you've done, Wendover.
STEVE: You started it, Kant.
MARK: It was both of you.
DON: You mean it was you two.
THE TRIO: (*To each other, in overlapping frenzy.*) It was you two, it was you two, no, it was YOU TWO!
   (*This time KATYA drowns their shouting with laughter.*)
STEVE: How can you laugh when we're all on the rack?
KATYA: Can you think of a better time for unrestrained glee?
MARK: (*Clutching her sleeve.*) You're still fond of me, though, Katya, aren't you?
KATYA: Yes, dear.
   (*DON hands her a handkerchief so she can blow her nose.*)
DON: And me?
KATYA: (*Blowing her nose.*) I suppose so.
STEVE: (*Shaking her.*) What about me?
MARK: (*Tugging at STEVE.*) Get your hands off her, you lecherous, backstairs sonovabitch.
STEVE: (*Whirling round on MARK.*) Lecherous, backstairs…?!
KATYA: That reminds me, Stephen, did you manage to put in the new staircase?
STEVE: No. The house is an absolute shambles without you. That's why Pip and I want you to stop making a sodding spectacle of yourself and come home.
KATYA: (*Amused.*) Pip's already bored with cooking, washing up and ironing for you, is she?
DON: If anyone's going to move into the cottage with you, Katya, it's me! I can't face going back to the YMCA.
MARK: I'll have to move in with you, too, Katya. I've no job now and no money.
KATYA: Oh don't. If you all keep going on like this, I'm bound to panic on an epic scale.
STEVE: So the question is, baby: which of us gets your lily-white mitt?

DON: Me!

MARK: No, me.

STEVE: Me. (*Softly.*) Please, luv.

MARK: Begging's cheating.

DON: So choose!

KATYA: (*Pacing in agitation.*) I'm so muddled and panicky, I don't know where I am. Or even who I am.

MARK: That's why you've got to choose one of us.

STEVE: Yeah, and you've got to choose now 'cause we're not going away 'till you do.

KATYA: I suppose the fairest thing to do in this booby-hutch of a situation is...well...

DON: Yes?

KATYA: Well, I'd better have...all three of you.

STEVE: At one sitting?!

KATYA: (*Laughing.*) Why not? I've always quite fancied the idea of a frenzied foursome.

(*With an abandoned flourish, KATYA flings open the door.*)

So – after you, messieurs.

MARK: (*Swallowing.*) You seriously going to let three of us make love to you at the same time?

KATYA: Isn't that what you want?

DON: Yes, but separately!

KATYA: I think it would be more democratic if there was an erotic scrummage.

STEVE: An erotic scrummage with you as the ball?

KATYA: I'd've thought balls – or lack of 'em – are more in your league, Stephen. But you don't have to join in if you don't want to.

STEVE: How can you be so fucking frivolous when your virtue is at stake?

KATYA: I find panic always overrides morality.

DON: Well, if this is the way you really want it, I'm game for a sexy scrum-down. (*Linking arms with KATYA.*) So let's have an orgy, sugar puff.

KATYA: (*Hesitant.*) You sure you're...up to it, Donald?

DON: Absolutely. I'm brimming over with lust.

KATYA: Help!

DON: You're not chickening out, are you?

KATYA: (*Now very jittery.*) No, oh no!

STEVE: If he's going to play Bacchus, I'm going to do my Dionysian bit.

KATYA: I didn't think a Greek inter-family gang-bang was your style, dear.

(*KATYA backs away from STEVE into MARK's arms.*)

MARK: It's not mine, either, but I'm not going to be a wallflower, and stand around and watch everyone else having fun but me.

KATYA: (*Fighting her way out of MARK's arms.*) What will your mother say?

MARK: I wouldn't do it to my mother. (*Ushering her towards the cottage.*) So – after you, Cleopatra.

STEVE: Yes, after you, Jezebel.

KATYA: Now wait a minute, I think we all should…

(*As KATYA dithers on the door step, PIP materialises out of the wood, with a shotgun.*)

PIP: …Put your hands above your heads before I blow your bleeding heads off.

KATYA: Oh Pip dear.

PIP: Don't 'Pip' me, you depraved hussy.

KATYA: Pip!

STEVE: So it was *you* who stole my shotgun.

PIP: Stay where you are, Dad, or I'll blast you out of your shoes. You're all disgusting animals. And that includes you, Mark.

KATYA: Have you been spying on us, dear?

PIP: Of course. Daughter like mother. No, keep your hands up and no tricks!

STEVE: Stop being melodramatic, luv, and gimme that thing before you shoot yourself in the foot.

PIP: I said keep your hands up, Dad, and shut it!

STEVE: Watch your mouth, daughter.

PIP: I'm not your daughter.

KATYA: Now don't be silly, dear.

PIP: Or yours. Like you two, I'm throwing restraint to the winds. From now on I'm a free agent. Well, as parents, you are both walking disasters. So I want to see the two of you squirm, like I squirmed back there watching you lot on heat.

STEVE: (*Edging forward.*) Now come on, sweetheart, you can't really believe that we were going to have...

PIP: '...An inter-family gang-bang'?

KATYA: Your father's right, dear. There's no way I could possibly have gone through with it.

DON: What d'you mean there's no way you could have gone through with it? I haven't been so turned-on since I lost my virginity.

KATYA: (*To PIP.*) Don't believe them, dear. It was all just a raunchy game.

PIP: (*Prodding her mother with the gun.*) No, you were going to go through with it, so you might as well admit it.

KATYA: I wasn't, dear. At least... (*Smiling.*) ...I hope I wasn't. Although once you miss the moment, you can never be really sure, can you?

DON: So you were leading us right up the garden path?

KATYA: Probably.

DON: Why?

KATYA: I panicked again.

(*JUDITH steps out of the wood, directly behind PIP.*)

JUDITH: You could've fooled me.

(*PIP swings round with the shotgun, and is momentarily blinded by JUDITH's torch.*)

PIP: Where did you spring from?

JUDITH: I've been watching you watching them playing funny-buggers, haven't I? Talk about ha-ha menagerie time.

(*Taking advantage of PIP being distracted, KATYA wrenches the shotgun out of PIP's hands. STEVE makes a grab for the gun but KATYA butts the barrel into STEVE's stomach, winding him.*)

KATYA: Hands off, Stephen.

STEVE: Gimme that!

KATYA: Belt up, you jerk, and back off.

(*JUDITH sneak ups behind her. KATYA whirls round.*)

And that includes you, Big Jude.

JUDITH: (*Backing off.*) Okay, okay, Wild Bill. Just give me my husband back and I'll beat a decorous retreat.

PIP: (*To her mother.*) And while you're at it, Mum, you can take your tarty claws off my apology for a boyfriend.

KATYA: I don't want any of you! I just want you all to get off my land before I blast you off it.

STEVE: Oh come on, luv, you wouldn't dare pull that trigger.

KATYA: You're probably right, 'hunbun' – unless you make me panic, of course. Then Heaven knows what I might do. (*Cheerfully.*) Because I certainly don't. So you'd better get the hell out of here right now before we find out. (*KATYA swings the rifle round wildly.*)

JUDITH: (*Ducking.*) Katya, be reasonable!

KATYA: (*Levelling the rifle at JUDITH.*) That's my last warning, Big Jude.

PIP: Mother, please!

KATYA: (*Continuing to swing the rifle wildly.*) Oh dear, I do think I'm about to panic. Yes, I'm sure I am!

STEVE: (*Backing away hastily.*) No, no, anything but that, sweetheart. We're off, aren't we, lads?

DON: You bet ya, but we'll be back.

MARK: First thing tomorrow morning.

STEVE: Then you'll have to choose one of us, luv.

DON: Or go through with the orgiastic foursome.

MARK: Either way, tomorrow'll be a day to remember. (*The three men back off into the trees. PIP turns to JUDITH as the MEN disappear.*)

PIP: What the hell are we going to do now?

KATYA: (*Levelling the gun at PIP and JUDITH.*) You're both going to piss off after 'em and leave me in peace.

JUDITH: I'm not going anywhere 'till I get my husband back.

PIP: And I want my boyfriend back. You can keep Dad.

KATYA: Thanks a million. (*KATYA laughs.*)

JUDITH: It's not funny, for Chrissakes.

KATYA: It certainly isn't anything else.

JUDITH: Katya, look, I know I've screwed up our friendship and our marriages but I am...well, truly sorry. I'll do anything to make amends. Anything! So long as you relinquish your hold on Don.
(*KATYA continues to laugh.*)
Well, you've got to admit that it's quite absurd that all three of 'em are in love with you at the same time!

KATYA: Not to mention very exhausting.

PIP: How can you be so callous, Mum?

KATYA: (*Impulsively hugging PIP.*) That's the very last thing I mean to be.

PIP: (*Hugging her mother back.*) Oh Mum! Let's be friends again, please.

KATYA: Nothing I'd like more in the world, dear. Just wish I wasn't so jumpy.
(*Abruptly PIP breaks away from her mother's embrace.*)
Now what have I said wrong?

PIP: Nothing. It's just so humiliating being cuddled by my deadly rival.

KATYA: I'm not your 'deadly rival', dear. Or yours, Judith.

JUDITH: Don't you want Don, then?

PIP: Or my Marky?

KATYA: I don't want any of 'em! I simply want to be left alone.

JUDITH: Then there's only one answer to all our problems.

KATYA: Which is?

JUDITH: You've got to make my husband fall out of love with you.

KATYA: I've got to do what?

PIP: Yes, and while you're at it, you can get Marky to fall out of love with you, too.

KATYA: What a delicious idea.

JUDITH: You mean you will help us to get our men back?

KATYA: With pleasure.

JUDITH: How you gonna do it?

KATYA: Simple. I shall send each of the Dynamic Trio a letter in which I shall make it absolutely clear that I refuse to see any of them for six weeks.

PIP: Then what?

KATYA: Then I shall inform them that after six weeks – if
  they continue to be under the erroneous impression that
  they're still in love with me…

PIP: Yes?

KATYA: …In that highly unlikely case, then they can all
  join me down here on March the twenty-fifth.

JUDITH: To do what exactly?

KATYA: Well, March the twenty-fifth is Lady Day.

PIP: So?

KATYA: So – I shall sit – as becomes a lady on her day of
  days, in royal state – and watch them while they duel for
  my lily-white hand.

JUDITH: 'Duel'?

KATYA: (*Beaming.*) Yes. And what's more, to the death. As
  an incentive I shall promise the one that survives the
  Trial by Combat – that's if any one does, of course – that
  he can have the very dubious honour of possessing my
  librarian's fraught little body.
  (*KATYA heads for the cottage but PIP prevents her going
  inside.*)

PIP: Oh for Christ sake, stop acting batty, Mum. No one
  duels today for anything. Except in the movies.

KATYA: (*Smiling.*) Yes, and isn't it boring? But if they're as
  crazy as you both think they are, on Lady Day they'll
  change all that, won't they?

JUDITH: You seriously expect 'em to fight it out with
  swords?

KATYA: (*Cheerfully.*) And pistols.

PIP: Swords and pistols?!

KATYA: Certainly. I haven't been studying the Russian
  Classics for nothing.

JUDITH: What happens if they kill each other?

KATYA: I'll find three more nutters and start again. On
  Mothering Sunday. Well, nighty-night, girls. Sleep tight.
  (*KATYA goes into the cottage and bolts the door from the
  inside. PIP bangs on the door.*)

PIP: Mum, you can't leave us like this. MUM!
  (*JUDITH laughs.*)

How can you laugh when it's the second time in six
weeks that she's pulled the same outrageous exit stunt?

JUDITH: Quit worrying, honey. There's no way I'm gonna
let my hubby get mixed up in a loony-tunes duel.

PIP: Those three wouldn't fight anyway. They haven't got
the guts.

JUDITH: They might; once your mother challenges them
to prove that they're 'real' men. Most guys are such
dumbdumbs that they'll fall for anything. But if they do,
I've a little surprise of my own that'll slice Katya's scalp
clean off.

(*JUDITH moves off, smiling.*)

PIP: (*Following her.*) You've got a plan to outwit her, then?

JUDITH: The beginnings of one. She did say she was
gonna get 'em to duel with pistols and *swords*, didn't she?

PIP: I don't see how swords are going to help us.

JUDITH: Believe me, kiddo, it takes more than one lady to
make a Lady Day.

(*Smiling, JUDITH disappears into the wood. PIP stares after
her perplexed.*
*There is a sudden violent splash in the lake. PIP whirls
round. There is another splash. PIP moves closer to the lake.
The splashing grows louder as the lights fade to blackout.*)

End of Act One

ACT TWO

Same setting.

Lady Day. 21 March.

The cottage is deserted and shuttered.

It is still dark. Just before dawn. There is a sharp ground frost and a keen wind blowing. Although it is late March, there are few signs that spring is coming. Winter still holds the lake in thrall.

The wind subsides. Shreds of cloud drift across the sinking moon.

A torch beam flickers among the trees in the wood. Moments later DON appears, incongruously dressed as a Russian Cossack, complete with fur hat and boots. He sports a tufted growth on his chin; his first attempt at a Cossack beard.

DON approaches the cottage.

DON: Katya, my darling, I'm here; and it's Lady Day!
    (*There is no response from the cottage. DON hammers on the door with his torch.*)
    Come on, my gorgeous one, open up and welcome your champion. I've even acquired the right gear for the duel. Greater love hath no man than to go to a theatrical costumiers to get fitted up to die.
    (*With a flourish, DON removes his hat and addresses the cottage in an appalling Russian accent.*)
    Allow me to introduce myself, Katerina. I am Dimitri Donovanovitch Kantoff, Imperial Cossack First Class and Duellist Extraordinaire, at your everlasting service.
    (*DON bows elaborately and almost knocks himself out on the corner of the trestle table. He yelps with pain. This is greeted by a WOMAN's laughter from the woods.*
    DON whirls round, only to be dazzled by the beam of a torch. DON responds by shining his torch at the shadowy figure.)
    That you, Katya?
FIGURE: 'Fraid not, my little babushka.

(*JUDITH steps into the fading moonlight. She is also incongruously dressed – but in a battered World War Two American flying jacket that is far too big for her. She is wearing jeans, furry flying boots, a pilot's leather hat and goggles.*)

DON: Bloody hell.

JUDITH: Quite. Though I still don't look as stupid as you, Comrade Dimitri Donovanovitch Kantoff.

DON: (*Embarrassed.*) Oh you heard my little Ruski tirade, did you?

JUDITH: Every 'Volga' word of it.

DON: Your puns are even worse than mine.

JUDITH: I know. Truth is, baby, I've missed you and your lousy puns so much that I've even started making up my own. Isn't that scary? (*Flinging her arms round his neck.*) You gotta come home, sweetheart, before I end up in the bunny-hutch.

DON: (*Disengaging himself.*) Judith, please.

JUDITH: I never begged you before, honey.
(*DON turns his back on her.*)
Look, I know it's taken me a long time to see the searchlight at the end of the tunnel. But, as Heaven is my witness, these last weeks I've done a helluva lot of thinking. And if there's one thing I've learnt from it all, it's that I've only ever loved one guy – and you just have the bad joss to be that sonovabitch.

DON: (*Breaking a twig off the apple tree.*) But how can I ever trust you again, Judith?

JUDITH: Give me another chance, baby. (*Pause.*) Please.

DON: Half this tree's dead.

JUDITH: Please, Don!

DON: I can't.

JUDITH: Oh c'mon, you're not really gonna fight a duel over Katya. You're a politician, for Chrissakes. No self-respecting MP has ever risked his life for love. It's a contradiction in terms.

DON: I've got to fight for something. I've no longer the stomach to wrestle with politics. And I can't bear compromising anymore. For the first time in my life, I'm going to make a stand for something and duel to the death.

JUDITH: That's romantic garbage, hunbun. People don't duel anymore. Except when they're road-raging on the motorway. So why don't you put your cute little arms around me and we'll have a Pax Juditho?

DON: (*Moving away.*) It's not that easy.

(*DON turns back to her. JUDITH is surprised to see that he is laughing.*)

JUDITH: What's so goddam funny?

DON: *You* are, in your furry flying boots, that goofball jacket and those ridiculous goggles. They're all much too big for you. Where did you find that gear, anyway?

JUDITH: It's all I've got left of my Dad.

DON: How morbid can you get?

JUDITH: There's nothing morbid about it. (*Indicating her flying jacket.*) I put it on because I felt in need of...I don't know...of being reassured, I suppose. And it's wonderfully snugly. (*Sidling up to him.*) Like you used to be, hun.

DON: (*Keeping her at arms' length.*) Why don't you go back to New York, Judith? There are lots of 'real' men on offer there to jump your bones.

JUDITH: D'you want the low down on why I had that ding-dong with Slobo Stevo?

DON: (*Turning his back on her.*) No!

JUDITH: 'Course you do. (*Pause.*) Face me, Don. I'm not scared of facing you.

(*DON does not turn round but snaps another twig off the tree.*)

That tree's not the only dead thing around here. Well, you think I haven't been aware that you've been panting for Katya's boobs since way back when.

DON: How'd you know? I mean...

JUDITH: 'Cause your eyes used to grow suction pads every time her mammaries flobbed into view. Your horniness was so blatant that, initially, I thought your puppy-dog slobbering was marginally cute. But then soon after you

started getting the hots for Katya, I noticed that you
stopped getting the hots for me. So it wasn't long before
I was praying that you'd either blow your wad in one big
bango session with her, or you'd find the nerve to leave
me and shack up with Katya permanently. 'Least that
way I'd know where I was – in Hell. Then I could try to
adjust my life accordingly. But, oh no, being the good
little Clacton-on-Sea Cromwellian voyeur that you are,
you just went on bulging at her boobs and slavering over
her bum. So one blustery afternoon last January, when
you were ranting in the Commons and Boobs was
working in the library, Stevo and I decided that we
might as well get drunk together. Which we did. Then
we got even drunker; until I was so smashed that
I...well, I suddenly swayed over to Stevo and tore his
shirt off.

(*DON stares at her.*)

Yeah, *he* looked kinda shook up, too. It certainly shook
me up. Then, to my amazement, Stevo burst out
laughing and shouted at the top of his voice the
immortal words: "Ooray! 'Oo-sodding-ray!" Then he
ripped off my blouse. Which, in turn, made me laugh.

(*DON's jaw drops.*)

(*Laughing in spite of herself.*) Well, it was pretty funny. Oh
I know it doesn't seem funny now, but at the time it was
hilarious. (*Controlling herself.*) Then after we'd finished
laughing, it seemed only logical for me to...well, for me
to rip his pants off. Which I did. This made him laugh so
hard, there were tears streaming down his face as
he...well, then he ripped my dress off. Then there was
nothing for it but for us to rip off everything else. Which
we did. 'Fact we had a pretty ripping time of it. Yeah, I
know; my puns make yours seem positively luminous.
But you gotta believe me, sugar, when I say I never
loved him. Not for one single moment. Or he me. We
just had insane rutting sessions. Problem was, once we go
into the way of it, it was like continually getting some
kinda erotic fix. And as we were both highly sexed by

nature, we went on with our little ding-dong 'till Katya blew us sky-high at the picnic. I know it was an unforgivably asshole thing to do to you both, but it's over now. For good. As God's my witness. (*Pause.*) Sweetheart, I'm more than willing to denigrate myself in front of you in any way you choose, so long as you give me one last chance. (*Pause.*) Don't I get anything for my confession? Even a slap in the mouth would be appreciated. (*Pause.*) Look, what the hell can I say to convince you that I'm gonna be faithful to you from now on? You gotta believe me when I tell you I've changed, for Chrissakes!

DON: No one changes, Judith. You said so yourself, remember, during our famous picnic: 'No matter your New Year's resolution, by Lady Day you'll be back where you were in the same over-flowing ashtray.'

JUDITH: So I was wrong! Absolutely wrong. But now I want to rectify things. Anyway, aren't you equally conning yourself?

DON: Me?

JUDITH: Yeah. You only hunger for Boobs 'cause she's illusive and full of Pantheistic bullshit. I dunno how you can stomach all her Nature schlock. What with screaming swans, grunting glissgliss and frigging ferrets, it's enough to make me wanna have a Technicolor yawn in the local vomitorium.
(*DON laughs.*)
It's not funny, Don, it's pitiful.

DON: See, you can't change. Not even for a moment.

JUDITH: Listen, Wordsworth, I like trees, lakes and all that lousy Greenpeace crap as much as the next guy, but I just don't burble on about it all the time.

DON: But that's your problem. (*Waving his arms at the lake.*) That sunrise doesn't fill you with wonder – when it should – because it's positively Wagnerian.
(*JUDITH laughs.*)
What the hell's funny about that?

JUDITH: The way you keep flapping your arms about's funny. Well, it looks like you're about to take off. It was your flapping about like that that screwed up most of your Election addresses. Who the hell wants Concorde as their MP?

DON: Oh go screw a tree!

(*DON charges off into the woods.*)

(*Calling.*) Katya? Katya! Where the blazes are you?

(*JUDITH rushes after him.*)

JUDITH: I didn't mean to upset you, honey. I just want you to land Concorde and come home with me now.

DON: (*Off.*) Katya? Hey, Katya?

JUDITH: (*Disappearing.*) Don, come home with me. Please!

DON: (*Fainter.*) Katya!

JUDITH: (*Off.*) Don!

(*From the opposite direction, we hear PIP calling.*)

PIP: (*Off, approaching.*) Mark! Mark!

DON: (*Now very faint.*) Katya!

JUDITH: (*Likewise.*) Don!

(*PIP appears.*)

PIP: (*Looking round her.*) Mark!

DON: (*Almost inaudible.*) Kat...ya!

JUDITH: (*Ditto.*) Don...!

PIP: MARK! (*Pause.*) Look, I know you're hiding around here somewhere.

(*No response. PIP bangs on the cottage door.*)

Mum, have you got Mark in there with you?

(*PIP tries the handle but the door is locked.*)

You're not satisfied with having Don and Dad, you've got to cradle-snatch as well. (*Banging on the door.*) And I won't tolerate it, Mum. D'you hear me?

(*PIP snatches up the axe from the wood pile. She is about to crash the axe through the window when MARK unexpectedly jumps out of the lean-to shed and restrains PIP. MARK is dressed in a bright red track suit. He is shivering with cold, and can barely speak because his teeth are chattering.*)

MARK: You're M-Mum's not in the cottage.

PIP: My poor darling, you're half frozen to death.

MARK: No, I'm c-completely f-f-frozen.

(*MARK claps his hands and stamps his feet, vainly trying to warm up.*)

PIP: Why were you hiding in the lean-to?

MARK: I've been on g-guard.

PIP: All night?

MARK: Since t-three this m-morning.

PIP: Oh you poor darling.

(*PIP tries to hug him but MARK backs away. He pulls a hip-flask of brandy from his trouser pocket and swigs down the dregs.*)

MARK: D-Don tried to sneak down here before me but I b-beat him to it.

PIP: (*In disbelief.*) You really love Mum that much?

MARK: Yes, I love her to b-bits and p-pieces. Like Lancelot worshipped Queen Guinevere.

PIP: (*Laughing.*) Queen Guinevere?

(*MARK extends his shivering right arm and peers along it.*)

MARK: I'm just praying that the c-cold won't make my p-pistol shake.

PIP: Oh come on, Mark, you're not really going to go through with this duelling nonsense, are you?

MARK: Don't touch me, Morgan Le F-Fay!

PIP: What?

MARK: You're not getting me into your lascivious t-toils again. Like Sir Galahad I've taken my first sacred v-vow.

PIP: You've done what?

MARK: And Katya's my Holy G-Grail.

PIP: Holy Grail? Sir Galahad. Morgan Le Fay? Can't you stop talking like something out of 'Morte D'Arthur'?

MARK: No! 'Cause I intend to make sure that it's going to be 'Morte de Donald' and 'Morte de Stephen'!

PIP: Oh grow up, for God's sake.

MARK: Says the cupi doll to the knight errant.

PIP: You may be a knight errant but I'm certainly no cupi doll. Not any longer. See, I've gone back to Sixth Form College to re-sit my 'A' Levels so I can go to University. Well, whatever happens, Mark, I'm definitely leaving home. For good. And if you had any sense, you'd do the same. Instead of standing here being a prize jerk with your teeth chattering like castanets. Especially as it's all for a woman who doesn't give a toss about you. (*Upset.*) I'm only going on like this, sweetheart, because…well, because I now realise that I really do love you, warts and all.

(*PIP seizes his hand but immediately MARK withdraws it.*)

MARK: If you love me as much as you say you do, Pip, why'd you turn me down when I proposed to you at the beginning of November?

PIP: Because I discovered that you'd already proposed to two of my best friends at the end of October! And now you've proposed to my mother as well. Well, you must admit it hardly gives a girl confidence in her man's emotional stability.

MARK: I can't help it if I've always wanted to get married, can I?

PIP: No, but do you have to marry every other girl you bump into?

(*MARK shrugs and shivers.*)

God, you're hopeless. And helpless. Oh for pity's sake, put this on. (*Handing him her coat.*) I can't bear the combination of you talking drivel and shivering while you're talking drivel.

(*PIP moves off.*)

MARK: Where you going?

PIP: To find Queen Guinevere.

MARK: (*Grabbing her sleeve.*) I won't let you stop our duel! I've been in training for weeks.

PIP: How d'you 'train' for a duel?

MARK: I practised with my little brother's crow-shoot, didn't I?

PIP: You men are unbelievable. You're nothing but great big, over-grown babies. On the one hand, there's Dad with his infantile Hornby train-set and his pathetic one-eyed teddy. Then there's Don who wants to turn into a swan so he can lay Leda. And now there's you; Sir Four-Eyes Prance-a-Lot, popping corks at plastic crows. Wherever you look, it's mind-boggling nursery time. To think you three are the Future of the West. No wonder the Third World's always pissed off with us.

(*STEVE steps out from behind the cottage, with his shotgun. PIP and MARK gasp in surprise.*)

STEVE: (*Calling out.*) Katya, come out from wherever you're hiding and let's get it over with.

MARK: (*Indicating the shotgun.*) You're not going to use that shotgun in the duel, are you?

STEVE: (*Grinning.*) You betya. And if I had a rocket-launcher, I'd use that, too. Or preferably a Centurion tank.

(*MARK snatches up the axe.*)

PIP: Mark, don't!

STEVE: Now that's what I call the perfect weapon against a shotgun.

(*PIP steps between them.*)

PIP: Now, both of you, stop behaving like funny-farm loonies. There isn't going to be a duel!

STEVE: Oh yes, there is!

(*JUDITH appears directly behind STEVE.*)

JUDITH: Oh no, there isn't. See, Tsarina Katya's fled over the State Line, and now she's probably running a circus for amorous midgets in Downtown Surbiton.

STEVE: Where'd you spring from?

(*DON materialises from the opposite direction, armed with a gigantic branch that he can barely carry.*)

DON: Same place as you, Stevo.

(*STEVE swings round to face DON with his shotgun.*)

PIP: Now, Dad, stop playing the fool and put the gun down.

JUDITH: No, Pip, let 'em fight each other. Nothing'd give me greater pleasure than to swab their battle wounds. I always find that men have such encouragingly low thresholds where pain is concerned.

STEVE: The question is: where the devil's our walking prize got to?

JUDITH: What d'you bet that she's pulling her smart-ass, picnic-routine again?

DON: You mean's she's set us up, and she's spying on us?

(*JUDITH grins and nods.*)

She wouldn't dare.

PIP: Wouldn't she?

STEVE: She bloody would!

MARK: And I've got a feeling she bloody is!

(*As if on cue, a rope snakes down from the cottage roof.*)

JUDITH: In the name of all that's Unholy!

(*Simultaneously a pair of Cossack boots, with their OWNER inside them, descends down the rope from the rooftop.*

It is, of course, KATYA, dressed in an eighteenth century Russian Hussar's uniform, complete with plumed beaver and thigh boots.

KATYA winks and waves as she lands gracefully on the trestle table. She has a large postman's bag tied to her back.)

KATYA: What a perfect dawn for a picnic.

JUDITH: (*To STEVE.*) What did I tell you? Another lousy set-up.

STEVE: Yes, Katya, where the hell've you been and why are you dressed up like a Cossack's dinner?

KATYA: This is how Catherine the Great dressed actually. In her tom-boy period.

PIP: What?

KATYA: She used to march around the Winter Palace in her Cossack uniform, and leer up at all her ex-lovers who were suspended in enormous gilded cages twenty feet above her. And every time the Empress passed them, she trilled: 'Pretty Polly, Pretty Polly. Pretty Polly.'

DON: You've been sitting on the roof spying on us, haven't you?

KATYA: Let's say, I've been surveying the frosty landscape and its infantile inhabitants from a draughty vantage point. (*Removing the sack from her back.*) So much so, I almost decided to give a miss to being Mother Christmas.

MARK: What've you got in the sack?

(*KATYA winks and grins.*)

STEVE: Don't just stand there like a sodding Cyclops, get off the table, then we can get on with the blood-bath in your honour.

KATYA: (*Shaking her head.*) Sorry, dear, but I rather like it up here. And it has the distinct advantage of allowing me to look down on your swarming little ant world.

JUDITH: How much of our conversation did you listen to?

KATYA: Very little. Unfortunately. I only wrapped myself around the chimney stack a few minutes ago.

MARK: How the hell did you get up there?

KATYA: Never heard of ladders? Spectacular night last night, wasn't it?

STEVE: What was so spectacular about it?

KATYA: Are you seriously telling me that you didn't watch last night's amazing storm?

DON: What storm?

KATYA: Must've been around midnight. Suddenly I woke up shivering. Something made me get out of bed and go to the window.

(Almost in a daze, KATYA climbs off the table. She moves down to the lake, re-living her memory. The others exchange concerned looks, questioning her sanity.)

Through the frosted glass, I watched this terrifying spectacle of thunder and lightning.

JUDITH: You can't watch thunder.

KATYA: If you have an imagination, you can. *(Staring at the lake.)* The storm was so vivid that I felt compelled to come out here and face its fury, which was foolhardy because the sky was screaming with electricity. The waves on the lake had crests of phosphorescent fire. Even the woods seemed to be on the move as the wind and the lightning flailed at the trees. And when you're confronted by such a scalp-crawling display of natural power, believe me, you feel remarkably insignificant. Especially when your only protection is a cotton nightie, and you're continually being almost blown off your feet. Yet at the same time I felt elated. It's hardly surprising. I mean, what a privilege it was to be allowed to applaud God's Own Orchestra, doing His Superior Version of Beethoven's Ninth. And the storm's climax! Wow! I thought my head would come right off. The cottage roof nearly did. The chimney still looks a touch squiffy. That's why I climbed up onto the roof just now to see how serious the damage was.

STEVE: There wasn't a storm last night. You must've dreamt it all.

PIP: And how!

KATYA: I assure you, my dears, there was a heaven of a storm. And not merely in my imagination. I'm still trembling from its impact.

(*STEVE snorts derisively.*)

I know, Stephen, in the immortal words of the Builder's Bard: 'It's just another bloody example of 'er pissin' feyness.'

JUDITH: Well, isn't it?

KATYA: No, Judith. The storm was as real as...that snowdrop. Mind, it is somewhat worrying to think that you lot could probably sleep through the ending of the world with scarcely an appreciative grunt.

DON: What's this got to do with why we're all gathered here at this unearthly hour?

KATYA: Yes, I've been meaning to ask you: why are you all trespassing on my land?

MARK: You know damn well you wrote and told us that if we three really loved you...

KATYA: Yes?

DON: ...We were to come down here on Lady Day, which is today...

KATYA: Yes?

STEVE: ...And we were to duel for your bonking body!

KATYA: You always express yourself so romantically, Stephen.

PIP: Mum, are you now denying that you wrote them those letters to set up this crazy duel?

KATYA: I'm not denying anything. But so much as happened to me in the interim, I'm afraid the duel must've slipped my mind. (*Smiling.*) Sorry.

JUDITH: What the hell can have happened to you to make you completely forget about three men fighting over who's going to screw you?!

KATYA: (*Continuing to smile.*) Hundreds of things, Judith.

MARK: Such as?

KATYA: Last night's storm. That was enough to put everything out of my mind. And there was the thrill of discovering a glade of aconites yesterday afternoon. Then last Wednesday I watched my first squirrel come out of hibernation. The day before that I glimpsed a vixen's silhouette against the sunrise. Three days ago there were two voles cavorting in the reeds...

STEVE: (*Shaking KATYA violently.*) Stop it, stop it, STOP IT!

KATYA: (*Disengaging herself.*) Stop what, Stephen?

STEVE: All this is Gardener's Weekly horse-shit. You're just messing us about again. So where are the pissing pistols for the duel?

KATYA: I don't have any pistols.

(*JUDITH, who has been rummaging in KATYA's Mother Christmas bag, lets out a whoop of triumph as she pulls out a black box which she opens with a flourish.*)

JUDITH: Unless my eyes deceive me, here are three braces of duelling pistols.

KATYA: You've no right to go sniffing around in my Mother Christmas bag.

JUDITH: And you've no right to be such a goddam liar.

(*STEVE snatches two pistols from the box.*)

STEVE: Take a butchers at the silver inlay. Truly magnificent.

MARK: Let me have a brace.

DON: (*Taking two pistols and sighting along them.*) I wish I had steady hands.

PIP: Stop 'em, Mum, for God's sake, stop 'em, before they fire the bloody things.

KATYA: Why should I? That's what I got 'em for.

JUDITH: You callous cow!

KATYA: Now be fair, Judith. All I have asked of any of you is that you allow me to live my life in peace and alone. So if a little judicious duelling is going to eliminate some of the trespassers on my property, you must surely see that I can't be held responsible.

MARK: (*Unsuccessfully trying to spin the pistols like a Western gunslinger.*) But you still agree that the one who's alive at the end of this shoot-out takes you to bed on the instant!

KATYA: Now there's no need to rush things, dear…

STEVE: We agree, darling, even if you don't. And if the winner has to ravish you in order to have his way with you, then I'll humping well ravish you.

KATYA: Oh for Chrissakes, shoot each other, ravish me and then shog off!

PIP: Mum!

DON: Yes, but…how the dickens are we going to have a three-way duel?

JUDITH: (*Taking charge.*) Simple. You put your backs to each other and create a human triangle. Then, on the signal, you each walk ten paces. Then you all turn round simultaneously and fire your pistols at your neighbours' chests. It's a piece of piss. Someone's bound to get killed, of course. Even if it's only one of the spectators.

MARK: Help!

JUDITH: Well, bang away, boys, 'cause I'm getting kinda peckish for some bacon and waffles.

PIP: Don't provoke 'em, Judith. You're only making things worse.

KATYA: No, Judith's right, dear. Let's have some fun for once. (*To the men.*) Well, don't just stand there jittering, my heroes; pot away at each other.

(*JUDITH sits on the table and swings her legs in anticipation.*)

STEVE: (*To DON and MARK.*) Ready, lads? Pistols cocked?

DON: (*Unsure.*) Think so.

KATYA: Yours cocked, Mark?

MARK: Everything about me's cocked!

STEVE: Right then, my boyos, let's get our backs together.
(*After a lot of shuffling, the men put their backs together and form themselves into a human triangle. They look ludicrous.*)

JUDITH: (*Laughing.*) If only you could see yourselves.
(*PIP clutches STEVE's sleeve.*)

PIP: You can't possibly go through with this, Dad.

STEVE: (*Shaking her loose.*) Shut up, lass, and duck down behind that tree.

MARK: (*Still trembling.*) This is better than the Gunfight at the OK Coral.

DON: (*Cod American.*) Yeah, a man's gotta do what a man's gotta do. (*To KATYA.*) Right, start the countdown.

KATYA: Look, boys, I've been thinking things over...

STEVE: That makes a change.

KATYA: I honestly don't think my body's worth all the pain that's coming your way.

JUDITH: Feeling's mutual, Boobs.

KATYA: For one thing I have a particularly large mole on my left breast.

MARK: Yes, I know. It's very sexy.

DON: You got that far, did you, Four Eyes!?

KATYA: And I've got an extremely crooked smile and the ugliest big toes in creation. Not to mention six very distinct stretch marks on my tummy.

STEVE: Oh shut it, will you? There are warriors here trying to concentrate.

MARK: Yeah, on eternity.

PIP: And Mum's slightly bow-legged, too, if you catch her at the wrong angle.

KATYA: I'm not bow-legged!

DON: Will someone give us the off before we burst out of our skins?

JUDITH: Sure thing, Clint. On your marks. Get set. Now don't rush it, remember. Ready... Steady...GO!
(*The men start measuring out their ten paces – in time to JUDITH's counting.*)
ONE.

KATYA: (*Ducking under the table.*) I was supposed to have given the signal.

JUDITH: Tough luck. TWO.

PIP: (*From behind the tree.*) This is total madness.

JUDITH: But what fun. THREE.

KATYA: I'm really not worth it.

JUDITH: True. FOUR.

STEVE: (*To KATYA.*) And you forgot to mention that your bum has dropped.

JUDITH: And how. FIVE.

DON: (*About his pistols.*) Knowing my luck, they'll backfire.

JUDITH: Bound to. SIX.

KATYA: (*Examining her bottom.*) My bum's not dropped!

JUDITH: But your boobs have. SEVEN.

MARK: Wish I knew how to fire these things.

JUDITH: You soon will. EIGHT.

PIP: Oh my God.

JUDITH: Quite. NINE.

STEVE: I'm really looking forward to this next bit.

JUDITH: Aren't we all? TEN!

> (*In unison the men stop and turn. They form the corners of a triangle. PIP covers her eyes. JUDITH drops flat on her face while KATYA continues to huddle under the table.*
>
> *The men level their pistols at their immediate neighbours. Then they close their eyes and fire simultaneously. The noise is deafening. PIP screams.*
>
> *When the smoke clears, the three men are still standing. PIP opens her eyes.*)

PIP: Thank God, thank God.

> (*Then MARK clutches his breast, drops his pistol and keels over. PIP rushes to him.*)
>
> Oh Marky, darling. (*Cradling MARK's head in her lap and screeching at her father.*) You've shot him, you mad bastard, you've shot my little boy.

STEVE: Rubbish. He's no more snuffed it than I have.

PIP: He hasn't?

DON: 'Course he hasn't.

DON / STEVE: (*In laughing unison.*) They were only bloody blanks!

PIP: You mean he's...

KATYA: (*Coming out from under the table.*) ...Just swooned, that's all.

PIP: Oh that's wonderful, just wonderful.

KATYA: You'd better loosen the poor darling's corsets and fetch him the smelling salts. By the by, how did you boys rumble my little ruse?

JUDITH: Same way as I did, you sneaky schmuck. We knew you couldn't possibly set up a blood-bath. You haven't the goddamn nerve.

> (*KATYA laughs. PIP smacks MARK's face to revive him.*)

KATYA: 'Least it's frightened some sense into one of them.

PIP: (*Still slapping MARK.*) Oh come back to me, dearest.
You're not dead, my hero, you just fainted.

MARK: (*Groaning as he come round.*) Am I in Heaven?

PIP: No, Sugar-plum. It's me; your very own Pipsy-poodle.

JUDITH: Yuck. It's enough to make you puke.

STEVE: (*Rubbing his hands in anticipation.*) Right, that's one
down, and one to go.

KATYA: Wasn't that lesson enough, Stephen?
(*STEVE picks up his shotgun and ejects the cartridges.*)

STEVE: I'm going to use this as a cudgel, Kant. So you
grab your branch and come in swinging.

DON: (*Squaring up to STEVE with his branch.*) Right, you've
asked for it, Big Mouth.
(*The men circle each other.*)

JUDITH: Now stop being total assholes! You'll do
yourselves a permanent injury.

DON: Silence, woman!
Now…. 'Lay on, Macduff,
And damn'd be him who first cries, "Hold, enough!"'
(*DON is about to launch himself at STEVE when KATYA
pulls two swords out of her Mother Christmas bag.*)

KATYA: (*Advancing between the men with the swords.*) As you
obviously want to seriously damage each other, why
don't you do it with some style?

DON: Swords!

KATYA: Epées actually. By kind permission of Colonel
Trumpington, who also furnished me with the pistols.

STEVE: God in hell.

DON: Have they got…buttons on the ends?

KATYA: (*Smiling.*) No. Just very sharp points.
(*STEVE picks up an epée and swishes it enthusiastically.*)

STEVE: Couldn't be better.

PIP: Dad, please don't go on with this, it's far too
dangerous.

KATYA: Grab yours, Donald, there's a good little
D'Artagnan.

JUDITH: (*Stepping between the two men.*) Don't you dare,
honey!

DON: I must say, I'd prefer to have a grenade.

KATYA: (*Handing DON a sword.*) Swords are more romantic.
And the whole thing will last that teensy-weensy bit
longer.

JUDITH: You can't make 'em go through with it, Katya.
One of 'em could lose an eye, or worse!

KATYA: Exciting, isn't it?

JUDITH: You're stark staring mad.

KATYA: (*Draping herself decorously on the table.*) I've never
had the odd gallon of blood shed over me before.
Except, of course, in hospital. But then, unfortunately,
that was mine. Well, *en garde, messieurs*; we haven't all
dawn.
(*The men are moving into their fencing positions when
JUDITH steps between them.*)

JUDITH: Put up your swords, you guys. This whole thing's
gone completely loco.

KATYA: Hasn't it just?

JUDITH: I said put 'em up, Don! I'm not having you
maimed for life merely to satisfy her perverse blood-lust.

PIP: Yes, walking out on us is one thing, Mum, but all this
duelling nonsense is sick and sadistic. And it's not like
you.

KATYA: True, dear. I used to be the sweetest and the most
understanding doormat in the Southern Counties, as long
as I agreed to cook cordon bleu nosh for you, wash up
the Crown Derby after, Hoover the house, bees wax the
Hepplewhite, polish the Georgian silver, do a Capability
Brown on the garden and play Einstein-cum-Ezra Pound
on your homework. 'Fact as long as there was an
inordinately tedious chore, habitually it had my name on
it. Mind, to be fair to your Popsy here, he wasn't satisfied
only to use me as a decorative drudge. No, he also
wanted to break my heart as he humped Big Jude here,
from the stables to the hen house and back again...

STEVE: (*Cutting in.*) We never did it in the hen house!

KATYA: And now he has the gall to pretend that he's
duelling with Donald to regain my love, when he's
simply doing it to save face. It's just another schoolboy

ı Lancastrian builder's machismo. Right, Juicey

ok, I've warned you not to mess with my

t that your ardent husband is any better. Donald
only claims that he loves me because he knows damn
well that there's no danger of me ever loving him back.

DON: That's a lie!

KATYA: Oh c'mon, admit it, Donald; your supposed love
for me is simply your latest Puritan ruse to avoid
climbing back into that apple-pie-bed marriage of yours.

DON / JUDITH: We don't have an apple-pie-bed marriage!

KATYA: Why don't you both own up to the truth for once?

JUDITH: Hark who's yelping.

KATYA: As the Virgin is my witness – on this her day of
days – I never asked any of you to invade my sanctuary.
But as you have forced yourselves upon me, you cannot
blame me for your own transformations.

STEVE: (*Laughing.*) Transformations?

KATYA: Yes. You've taken upon yourselves the
characteristics of the predators in these woods. In the
process you've turned me into a predator, too. So – as far
as I'm concerned – if you want to fight, fight. If you
want to make love, make love. Do what the blazes you
like, so long as you leave me out of it. I just want to be
alone. Is that too much to ask? (*Suddenly near to tears.*) I
promise I won't interfere in any of your lives ever again
if only you'll take your claws out of me. Make up your
minds what you want to do with yourselves; then do it,
do it! But for pity's sake, do it SOMEWHERE ELSE!

STEVE: Well, don't just stand there like a castrated
cockroach, Kant. Either fight me or leave the field like
the snivelling yellerbelly you are.

DON: (*Squaring up to STEVE.*) No bilious berk of a builder
calls me yellow!

KATYA: The Virgin give me strength.

(*The men go into their en garde positions.*)

PIP: Stop it, stop it, both of you, stop it!

(*As the men are about to duel, JUDITH picks up DON's branch and knocks the sword out of DON's hand.*)

DON: Why the hell did you do that?

KATYA: Yes, if they want to kill each other, let 'em kill each other. 'Least that way I'll get some peace.

JUDITH: (*Picking up DON's sword.*) You're sick in the head, Katya.

KATYA: So you keep telling me.

STEVE: Give Don his sword back, Jude. This is men's work.

JUDITH: (*To STEVE.*) Rubbish. Now gimme your sword, Fairbanks Junior.

STEVE: Not a chance.

JUDITH: If you don't, you'll have to fight me, punk. And I fight Brooklyn dirty. So hand it over before you get hurt.

STEVE: (*Amused.*) Okay, okay.

(*STEVE throws the epée to JUDITH who catches it easily.*)

PIP: Thank God someone's got some sense.

STEVE: This whole foul-up's your fault, Katya, you know that?

JUDITH: You never spoke a truer word. (*To KATYA.*) Catch, Pussy Galore.

(*JUDITH throws one of the swords to KATYA who catches it easily.*)

Now jump off of your throne and get *en garde*, Boobsypooh.

KATYA: I'm not going to fight you, Judith.

JUDITH: You've no choice.

KATYA: I won't fight you, and there's no way you can make me.

JUDITH: Really? Then howsaboutdis for openers?

(*JUDITH slashes KATYA's Hussar hat off her head.*)

KATYA: I hired that hat!

JUDITH: If that's the only thing that comes outta this with torn fur, you'll be a lucky son of a gun.

KATYA: I'm still not going to fight you, Judith.

JUDITH: Typical. The lady's not only a trouble-stirring, lying daughter-of-a-bitch with drooping tits...

KATYA: My tits don't droop!

JUDITH: …But she's also so inadequate as a woman and a lover that she allows her best friend to straddle her husband right under her prim little conk.

KATYA: (*Leaping off the table.*) You Yankee whore!

PIP: Oh don't you two start, for God's sake!

JUDITH: And to top it all, little Convent Knickers here has to dress up as Catherine the Great to cover up the fact that she's got the guts and backbone of a squashed mollusc!

(*JUDITH jabs KATYA with her sword.*)

KATYA: OWWWW! (*Lunging back at JUDITH.*) You foul mouthed pole cat!

JUDITH: (*Laughing and parrying.*) That's more like it, Kate the Great.

(*They start to fight in earnest.*)

KATYA: Up yours, Jude the Lewd.

(*KATYA lunges again. JUDITH parries brilliantly. Then JUDITH lunges. KATYA parries. Both women are surprisingly good swordswomen. The men gape on in amazement as the duel becomes increasingly more spectacular.*)

PIP: (*Catching her father's sleeve.*) You're not going to just stand there and let them stab one another, Dad, are you?

STEVE: Why not? Women fighting are very sexy.

PIP: Dad!

STEVE: Prefer 'em fighting naked in mud, of course. But then as your mother says I'm not much of a romantic.

PIP: You're not much of anything, Dad. Can't you stop 'em, Don?

DON: Not a chance. When my wife bares her fangs, woe betide anyone who gets their neck in the way. (*Shouting to JUDITH.*) What a brilliant parry, Crude Jude.

STEVE: (*Also shouting encouragement to KATYA.*) That's it, luv, press home your advantage. Talk about a raunchy turn-on.

MARK: Yes, it's a real arouser, isn't it?

STEVE: And how.

DON: True, it's not often you see ladies duelling for the honour of climbing into the gentlemen's beds.

JUDITH: (*Now in retreat.*) You nearly had my nipple off, you doxy!

KATYA: (*Pressing home her advantage.*) Well, you've just slashed open my jerkin, you great gherkin.
(*The girls are now fighting their way round the tree, à la the Three Musketeers.*)

MARK: Must say it is highly erotic. I especially love the way Katya wheels her sword around her bonce. Gives me such an eyeful of cleavage.

PIP: Mark!
(*KATYA leaps onto the table. JUDITH slashes wildly at her legs. KATYA leaps over the blade, à la Errol Flynn.*)

STEVE: That's it, luv, keep doing the Highland Sword Dance. Then jump on the old bag and flatten her.
(*KATYA leaps off the table, forcing JUDITH to retreat.*)
Yeah, yeah, girl; now pig-stick the Brooklyn Bomber.

DON: Not a chance. My Jude's too good. She makes Errol Flynn look like Fatty Harbuckle.
(*Both women are now panting but enjoying themselves as they hack at each other.*)

JUDITH: Where the devil did you learn to fight like this?

KATYA: I played Viola in 'Twelfth Night' when I was in the Sixth Form. I had to duel with Sir Toby Belch in the last Act. (*Now retreating.*) You're not so arthritic yourself. Where did you learn?

JUDITH: At High School where I played Sir Toby.
(*KATYA laughs and JUDITH all but stabs her.*)

KATYA: Hey, watch it! You almost had me then.
(*They both lunge at the same time. Their sword hilts lock together. With their free hands, the women wrestle each other. The men continue to yell partisan encouragement.*)

STEVE: Go on, luv, give her a forearm jab in the tits.

MARK: No, kick her in the bum.

DON: (*To JUDITH.*) Knee her in the crotch.

KATYA: (*Still wrestling with JUDITH.*) Certainly not. We're lady duellists, aren't we, Judith? Not Clacton-on-Sea Mafia. (*To JUDITH.*) Oooh you firking faghag, you've just put your great hoof on my corn!

JUDITH: No mother fucker calls me a firking faghag!

(JUDITH grabs KATYA by the hair and forcibly swings KATYA round. KATYA yelps and shoves the hilt of her sword into JUDITH's midriff, momentarily winding her. KATYA lets out a yell of triumph and lunges – thrusting her sword into JUDITH's armpit.)

(To KATYA.) You insane bitch.

(Horrified at what she's done, KATYA pulls the sword out of JUDITH's arm and hurls the sword into the trees. The others are so stunned by what has happened that for a moment no one speaks.

JUDITH crumples to her knees. DON rushes to support JUDITH.)

DON: Don't worry, baby, we'll have you in hospital in no time.

JUDITH: No need, hunbun, it's only a scratch. But the shock made my knees buckle. Hold me, just hold me.

KATYA: God in Hell, I could've killed you.

DON: *(To KATYA.)* You sure it's only a scratch, baby?

JUDITH: I'm fine, honey, believe me. But I love you holding me.

KATYA: Judith, I'm so sorry. You've no idea how sorry I am.

JUDITH: Stop lying to yourself, bitch. You know damned well you planned everything, didn't you? Down to the last detail.

KATYA: In a way. But most of my so-called planning was sheer panic. And it was mixed up with a morbid urge for revenge. Well, understandably I wanted to make you all grovel, like you'd made me grovel. But now I realise I shouldn't have 'cause Pip and Mark, and you, Don, were really quite blameless. Trouble was, I was so muddled and upset that I went out of my way to make you feel as empty and discarded as I felt. Recently I've been very lonely, and often felt totally lost. The last couple of weeks, the cold and the long nights have really got through to me. Just like you said they would, Stephen. Though until then it was pretty exhilarating hiding behind pine trees and hooded owls and...

PIP: …Glissgliss?

KATYA: Yes.

DON: And the grappling pike.

KATYA: Don't rub it in.

MARK: Don't forget the Puss Moth pupa.

KATYA: How could I? But then I've always been an expert at hiding behind things. If I'm not submerging myself in Nature, I'm losing myself in Goggling Gogol and Poncing Pushkin. 'Fact when I think things through – and until this moment I don't seem to have thought anything through properly – one of the reasons I've hidden myself down here by the lake is to make a point. So again you're right, Judith – damn you – because living is not about making points. Living's about…well, it's about…God only knows what it's about! I certainly don't. Listen to me. I'm doing it again, sounding off when I almost killed you.

(*To everyone's amazement, JUDITH laughs and jumps to her feet.*)

JUDITH: Bullshit. There's no way you could've killed me. 'Fact I've never felt better in the whole of my life.

KATYA: What?

JUDITH: 'Fact your sword didn't even scratch me.

(*JUDITH opens her flying jacket to reveal…*)

STEVE: A bloody fencing jacket!

JUDITH: (*Laughing.*) Not to mention the thickness of this gorgeous lamb's wool lining, plus the toughness of the leather and three inordinately heavy sweaters.

KATYA: (*Amazed.*) Then you're not hurt at all?

JUDITH: 'Course not. I had no intention of being. I didn't wear my Dad's old flying gear merely for sentimental reasons. See, I planned this little duel.

DON: You planned it?

JUDITH: You bet ya. I wasn't gonna let you get yourself killed, hunbunch. I knew there was only one person who could sort out Queen Boudicca here, and that was me. So in order that I didn't end up in the local morgue, I got myself some serious body armour. I'm the hard-nosed,

street-wise, Brooklyn Bomber, remember? Not some
dumbdumb knight from the Round Table.

KATYA: You mean...when I thought I was setting you up,
you were setting me up?

JUDITH: Something like that. You must admit it makes a
change.

KATYA: Well, I'll be...you sly old bag.

(*JUDITH laughs. The others join in.*)

MARK: (*To KATYA.*) So you've been caught in your own
Lady Day trap.

JUDITH: And by a lady who aint no lady.

DON: Question is...where the hell do we all go from here?

KATYA: (*Mischievously.*) If you come back in six weeks'
time, we can have an action replay.

PIP: Now don't start all that again, Mum.

STEVE: Yeah, just come home quietly, luv, like a good little
prodigal.

JUDITH: (*To DON.*) Same goes for you, Super Stud.

PIP: (*To MARK.*) And you, Sir Galahad.

(*MARK, DON and KATYA exchange looks.*)

Well, are you coming, Marky?

MARK: Maybe...but I'm not going to propose marriage
again.

PIP: You bet your life you're not. You've got a helluva lot
of growing up to do, my lad, before I dare risk anything
as dodgy as us getting married.

JUDITH: (*To DON.*) How's about you, big boy? You gonna
saddle up your horse in my corral?

DON: I suppose you need someone to put you out to grass.

JUDITH: (*Rushing in DON's arms.*) Oh Donnypooh, my
cutesy Donnypooh.

KATYA: Now that's what I call real yuck.

STEVE: What about us, luv?

KATYA: What about us?

STEVE: (*Going to her.*) Well, I thought we might...

KATYA: (*Moving away from him, down to the lake.*) Won't
work, Stephen.

STEVE: (*Following her.*) Let's give it one more go, lass.
Please.

(*Pause.*)

PIP: Oh please, Mum. Please!

KATYA: (*After another pause.*) Alright. We'll have one last try, Stephen. But if it even starts to go wrong again, I want out – instantly. So, I'll give you until...

STEVE: ...Lady Day next year, I know. If it hasn't worked out by then, sweetheart, you'll have my blessing to have it off with every sodding pine tree in this wood.

KATYA: How'd you know I was going to choose Lady Day?

STEVE: Your little surprises are always so predictable, luv. Well...nearly always. Pip, why don't you and Lover Boy nip home and rustle us up some breakfast? All this duelling's set my taste buds on edge.

PIP: Then why don't you nip home, Dad, and do some breakfast-rustling yourself?

MARK: (*Taking PIP's hand.*) Yes, and then you can bring it up to us, Mr Wendover. In bed.

STEVE: You idle, randy little git!

(*Laughing, MARK and PIP run off into the wood. DON and JUDITH also move to go.*)

JUDITH: (*To KATYA and STEVE.*) Well, 'bye, you guys. See you around sometime. Like next Lady Day. Maybe.

KATYA: (*Laughing.*) Quite. Sorry again for everything, Judith. Well...I'm almost sorry.

DON: (*Awkwardly shaking hands with KATYA.*) Yes well... thanks for the experience, Katya. It hurt a lot...but as I'm a true masochistic Englishman, I must say I loved every moment of it.

(*DON goes off abruptly into the trees. JUDITH runs off after DON.*)

JUDITH: (*Off.*) Don honey – hang on! DON!

STEVE: (*To KATYA, once they're alone.*) D'you think they'll be able to re-assemble their marital jigsaw puzzle?

KATYA: D'you think we will?

STEVE: Well, I certainly promise to try and get rid of all my bad habits.

KATYA: Don't promise, Stephen. Or try. Just get rid of them.

(*KATYA opens the cottage door.*)

STEVE: (*Grinning in anticipation.*) Oh I see; you fancy us doing a fertility rite in your little hut to celebrate the Prodigal's Return?

KATYA: Later perhaps. There's no hurry.

STEVE: Speak for yourself!

KATYA: I am. And from now on I always will. So why don't you let me show you around your new home?

STEVE: New home?! This clapped-out joint?

KATYA: Oh did I forget to mention it? As an integral part of your getting rid of your innumerable bad habits, you will start by moving into my cottage on probation.

STEVE: On probation?

KATYA: And you will fit your life around mine for a change.

STEVE: Now hang around...

KATYA: You can 'hang around' as much as you like. But as the old rhyme says:
'The Lady must have her way on Lady Day,
And you must obey the lady in every way
Because from now on, every day is Lady Day.'
So the choice is yours, Stephen.
(*Laughing at STEPHEN's obvious discomfort KATYA goes into the cottage, leaving the door open.*)

STEVE: Katya, be reasonable... Look, darling, we've got to talk this through. (*Coing into the cottage.*) Katya, stop laughing. KATYA!
(*Above him, there is a deafening beat of wings, accompanied by the honking cries as several swans fly over the cottage. There is the skirr of splashing water as the swans land on the lake.*
Moments later, KATYA runs out of the cottage down to the water's edge.)

KATYA: Stephen, look! The swans have come back. Spring can't be far behind.

STEVE: (*Appearing in the doorway.*) But when it comes, will we be able to keep up with it?

KATYA: As my mother always used to say: 'We have two chances.'

(Laughing uncertainly STEVE joins KATYA by the lake. A blackbird sings jubilantly in the woods as the lights fade.)

The End

REVELATIONS

a play

Characters

VICAR

JED THOMAS

ROB BULFORD

MAGGY BULFORD
his wife

BETH HAXTON

SANDRA WENLOCK

STRANGER

SIMON

Revelations was first performed at Roberts Theatre, Grinnell, Iowa, USA on 24 April 1986, with the following cast:

VICAR, Tim Black

JED THOMAS, Glenn Martin

ROB BULFORD, Ian Roberts

MAGGY BULFORD, Linda Levinson

BETH HAXTON, Laura Maly

SANDRA WENLOCK, Ingrid Scott

STRANGER, David Pinner

SIMON, Rich Beck

Director, Jan Czechowski

Designer, Jan Czechowski

Lighting, Cari Norton

Costume, Sarah Garrett

PART ONE

Scene 1

St Mary's graveyard. Seafall Village. On the bleak east coast of anywhere.

Time: the present. Early Spring.

Dawn seeps through storm-riven clouds, gilding the gravestones that line the edge of the cliff like rotten teeth. A mossed bench overlooks the graveyard.

Then the light dawn is all but extinguished, and the relentless wind reigns supreme.

As the wind continues to predominate, the VICAR, forty-five, wiry, with a well-kept beard and muffled in a black cassock, appears breathless in the cold. He is dragging a splintered beam from the church roof, with the assistance of JED THOMAS, who is a thirty-five year-old school teacher. JED has prematurely receding red hair and stooping shoulders.

The men lay the beam against several others, then pause for breath, staring back at the church.

VICAR: (*Pinched with cold.*) What a way to start Lady Day.
JED: (*Examining another hole in his woollen gloves.*) That what today is?
VICAR: (*Nodding.*) When the Virgin got herself enunciated, God bless her. Unfortunately it's only going to be remembered as the day the church roof blew off.
    (*JED moves to the edge of the graveyard and peers over the cliff.*)
JED: Our forefathers were not only dumb enough to come to these godforsaken parts, Vicar, but they had the vacuous temerity to build Seafall on the edge of a cliff, so it's hardly surprisin'...
    (*The wind gusts ominously.*)

VICAR: Come away from there, Mr Thomas. The wind'll
blow you off.

JED: No chance.

VICAR: That bit of cliff could easily give way.

JED: (*Not moving.*) Chunk of it already has. (*Grinning.*) How
many headstones d'you reckon went over?

(*Hesitantly the VICAR joins JED on the cliff's edge.*)

VICAR: Good half dozen. (*Crossing himself.*) God rest their
souls.

JED: Couple of crosses down there, too. (*Pointing.*) On that
wet patch o' sand.

VICAR: That's a skull, isn't it?

JED: (*Peering.*) Can't tell from here. Fair scatterin' of bones,
though.

(*Again the wind gusts, prompting the VICAR to edge away
from the cliff.*)

VICAR: What a tragic indignity to have your skeleton
strewn all over the beach.

(*The wind increases in velocity.*)

Wind's getting worse by the minute.

JED: That's how last night's storm started.

(*The VICAR whirls round as more tiles are blown from the
church roof and shatter on the flagstones.*)

VICAR: (*Calling out.*) Mrs Haxton, watch out! Maggy, get
her away from there!

MAGGIE: (*Off.*) What's the matter, Vicar?

VICAR: That beam! No, the one balanced on the plinth. It's
slipping!

BETH: (*Off, coughing.*) We can see it, Vicar. No need to get
your knickers in a twist.

(*The VICAR shakes his head, then rubs his eyes.*)

JED: Don't worry about Beth. She'd survive a hurricane.

VICAR: Still can't understand why the lightning destroyed
the altar, and not the steeple. And the main entrance and
belfry were scarcely touched.

(*JED smiles.*)

What's so funny? You should've called the fire brigade.

JED: The wind blew all the bloody phone lines down.
Anyway, it's our cottages worries me. Another storm like

last night's, an' the rest of the cliff'll give way. And next time our homes'll go with it.

VICAR: It'll take more than a storm, surely?

JED: The Sunken Village is only around the bay.

VICAR: Yes, but that was caused by the worst storm this century.

JED: Last night's was close to it in its fury, believe me.

(*JED rolls a cigarette and offers the VICAR his tobacco tin.*)

VICAR: No, thanks. Given them up for Lent.

JED: (*Pointing with his toe.*) Seen that crack there? That goes right the way inland, along the High Street, under Mrs Haxton's front door step, under mine, an' the Bulfords. It's only two or three yards wide of Old Simon's place end of the row.

VICAR: Yes, but the way the Sunken Village came about was...

JED: (*Overriding him.*) Much the same way. My parents used to live in the village thirty years ago until that bitch of a storm. They only just got out o' their cottage in time. They saw the storm wrench most of the cliff away. Some of the cottages were literally ripped in half. Whole walls twisted and buckled like meltin' toffee before they crashed down into the waves. That's why my parents came up here to live in Seafall.

VICAR: (*Smiling.*) Surely they'd had enough of living on top of a cliff?

JED: Outsiders don't understand anythin'.

VICAR: I try to understand the needs of each of my parishes.

JED: Really? Then you should realise that it was because these cottages are perched on the edge of the cliff that my parents came to live here. Home from home, see. (*Grinning.*) D'you think the spire'll come down next time?

(*There is a gust of wind.*)

VICAR: If it keeps blowing like this, God knows what will happen. 'Least I hope He does.

JED: God's got nuthin' to do with it, Vicar.

VICAR: (*Laughing.*) Now don't start on that old hobby-horse of yours again, Mr Thomas.

(*The VICAR goes back to the church.*)

JED: (*Calling after him.*) I mean it! 'Fact I wish the storm had blown the whole of that god-box into the sea. Then I could've purged the villagers of their pathetic reliance on the 'hereafter' while there's still time.

(*Laughing, the VICAR re-appears, carrying part of the damaged lectern. Oblivious, JED sits on a head stone to re-light his cigarette, blown out by the wind.*)

'Cause, believe me, Vicar, until the masses are purged of your so-called 'hereafter', I shall never be able to organise 'em for the here and now.

VICAR: (*Laughing in disbelief.*) The 'masses'?

JED: Ay, the masses.

VICAR: Seafall's only got a population of thirteen, and four of them are kiddies.

JED: (*Still trying to re-light his cigarette.*) Their lack of proletarian consciousness is no laughing matter.

VICAR: If you believe that, why are you helping us to clear up the church?

JED: (*Kicking one of the beams.*) 'Cause I can use all the beams up at my school.

VICAR: How?

JED: (*Grinning.*) In my wood-work classes, 'course.

(*JED goes off.*)

VICAR: (*Amused.*) You're incorrigible, Mr Thomas.

(*Following JED off.*) Rob, for pity's sake, put that beam down!

MAGGY: (*Off, approaching.*) You tell him, Vicar. (*To ROB.*) You could hurt yerself bad, luv.

(*ROB BULFORD, a moustached giant in his late forties, effortlessly shoulders a huge beam into the graveyard – even though he is blind. MAGGY, his wife, a sensuous, flaxen-haired woman in her mid-thirties, tries to guide ROB between the gravestones.*)

ROB: (*Shaking her off.*) Let me be, wife! Me toes are open-eyed, even if me skull ent.

MAGGY: Rob, you'll fall over the edge!

(*The VICAR helps MAGGY to restrain ROB.*)

VICAR: Let me give you a hand with that, Mr Bulford.

ROB: (*Tossing the beam down.*) I can manage.

VICAR: Why doesn't anyone ever listen to me?

ROB: Beginnin' to get through to you, too, ent it, Vicar?

VICAR: (*Trying to laugh.*) What makes you say that?

ROB: Can hear yer heart racin' from here.

(*JED brings in a box of slates.*)

VICAR: It's all so inexplicable. Only four miles up the coast, we haven't had a storm for over three months.

ROB: (*Lighting his pipe.*) Since the autumn we've 'ad nuthin' but storms.

(*JED grins.*)

MAGGY: Were much the same last March.

JED: (*Enjoying himself.*) An' the March before. (*Offering the VICAR a cigarette paper.*) Sure I can't tempt you?

VICAR: No! (*Recovering his good humour.*) Thank you, Mr Thomas. I'm not saying that the weather's been particularly brilliant in my other parishes, you understand. But here in Seafall, by any standards, it's been absolutely... I don't know...

JED: (*Mischievous.*) ...Diabolical? (*Winking.*) Only in the figurative sense, of course.

VICAR: Of course. (*Now agitatedly pacing.*) What's so disconcerting is that every time I drive off the main road to come up here, the temperature seems to drop in the space of less than a mile or so. And the wind springs up out of nowhere. (*To JED.*) Can you explain it? You're the intellectual.

JED: (*Laughing.*) One thing's certain, it's not a coincidence, Vicar. Perhaps 'him up there' is tryin' to tell you something – if 'he' was up there, of course – which 'he' isn't. But what 'he's' trying to tell you, is – you're not wanted around here, Vicar. What's more, it's not goin' to be long before the rest of them around here *tell* you that you're not wanted. An' when they do, you an' your god are over. Then the villagers'll start tryin' to save themselves, instead of them just waitin' for your imaginary christ to jump off his cross an' save them.

(*JED goes back to the church.*)

MAGGY: Don't mind his rantin', Vicar. He can't help it. He's a teacher.

VICAR: (*Laughing.*) I know, Maggy. But it is the third day of spring, and there's not even a hint of a crocus, let alone a daffodil.

ROB: It's the wind. Blasts everythin' it touches.

(*MAGGY wraps her husband's scarf tightly around his neck.*)

VICAR: What are you going to do if the wind blows off the rest of the top-soil?

MAGGY: Not much we can do, is there? 'Cept live off the State.

ROB: (*Coughing on his pipe.*) An' get cancer, 'course.

(*ROB sits on a tombstone to knock out his pipe.*)

VICAR: But if we have another wet summer, the few crops that do germinate will rot in the ground before they can be harvested. Then what will you do?

MAGGY: (*Joining her husband on the tombstone.*) Your guess is as good as ours, Vicar. (*Cheerfully.*) Even the gulls fly inland most days now 'cause our fishing's nigh on dead. What with them foreign factory ships, and them tankers dumpin' their oil in the sea.

VICAR: Quite! So how can you both just sit there on Betty Ramsbottom's head philosophising?

ROB: (*Surging to his feet and grabbing the VICAR's lapels.*) Don't mock us, Vicar!

VICAR: Careful, Rob. I have one moveable vertebra as it is.

ROB: Our world's goin' to be blown into the sea!

MAGGY: (*Trying to pull ROB away from the VICAR.*) 'T'isn't his fault, luv.

ROB: We're DAMNED here in Seafall. Damned, I tell you!

VICAR: Damnation's got nothing to do with it.

ROB: (*Shaking his head.*) Were God's Own Lightnin' set fire to His Own Altar, and hurled them graves over the cliff.

MAGGY: Don't start, luv.

VICAR: God has nothing to do with it. These disasters are...

ROB: (*Interrupting.*) ...Acts of God! 'Cause God's done with us here in Seafall, an' us are for the drownin'.

(*The VICAR is distracted by activity around the church.*)

VICAR: (*Calling off.*) Sandra! Mrs Haxton! Get away from there! That beam's unsafe, I tell you.

BETH: (*Off.*) So are our cottages? So what?
(*There is a fierce gust of wind. A beam in the church roof can be heard thudding onto the flag stones, followed by the clatter of falling tiles.*)

VICAR: (*Rushing off.*) God help us!

JED: (*Off, laughing.*) That'll be the day.

BETH: (*Off.*) 'S'all right, Vicar, it missed us.

VICAR: (*Off.*) Clearing the church is men's work, ladies, men's work.

BETH: (*Off, laughing.*) Well, we *are* the men around here, Vicar; didn't you know?

ROB: (*Calling out.*) Then you're the first man with pink bloomers, Beth 'Axton.

BETH: (*Off, coughing and laughing.*) You Peepin' Tom!

MAGGY: (*To ROB.*) How d'you know her bloomers are pink, Rob?

ROB: (*Grinning.*) Got a long memory of a certain washin' line on windy days, ent I?
(*ROB makes to follow the VICAR off but MAGGY restrains him.*)
Stop clutchin' me, will you?

MAGGY: If another of them tiles slips, it'll slice off yer head!

ROB: (*Shaking his head.*) I've a sixth sense 'bout such things, woman.

MAGGY: Pity yer sixth sense didn't stop you gettin' blinded!

ROB: I got meself blinded tryin' to net 'nough fish to keep you an' the kids!

MAGGY: I know, luv… (*Trying to take his hand but he snatches it away.*) Why'd you make me say such terrible things?

ROB: Maybe you say 'em 'cause you mean 'em.

MAGGY: You've no idea how hard it is for me lookin' after the boys an' the cottage on me own. An' I have to earn most of the money.
(*JED comes in with some more tiles.*)

ROB: You think I like bein' blind, woman!

MAGGY: (*To ROB, but she is aware of JED.*) Only tryin' to protect you.

JED: That church is a death house.
(*JED stares at MAGGY.*)

MAGGY: Don't turn away, sweetheart.

ROB: Why don't you do some'at useful for once, gal? An' give our lusty teacher what he's hankerin' for.

JED: (*Taken aback.*) And what's that?

ROB: Don't need eyes in me head to know how you're always gawkin' at my Maggy.

MAGGY: Rob!

ROB: You're strippin' her right now, under them droopy lids of your'n.
(*Furiously JED slicks his hair forward; it is one of his mannerisms.*)

JED: Stop makin' a fool of yourself.

ROB: (*Grinning.*) Slickin' them wisps of hair forward won't stop the rest fallin' out.

JED: You evil-mind…

MAGGY: (*Overriding him.*) Take no notice of him, Jed. He don't mean half he says. Just when he's got one of these moods on, he…
(*JED goes off.*)

ROB: (*Massaging his forehead.*) So dark in here. Can't help tormentin' meself. Laugh is, I can't abide self-pity.

MAGGY: (*Wrapping the scarf round his chest.*) You're shiverin', sweetheart. Let me take you home.

ROB: No. Contented where I am. I feel… I dunno…a kind o' kinship with the wind. An' the fact there's no flowers out yet. Even the buds've got ice in their hearts. Sounds morbid, dunnit? (*Chuckling to himself.*) God must have a marvellous sense of humour. Sometimes He's such a clever-clogs, us poor devils can't be sure whether He an' the Devil aren't one an' the same. It shows how damned this village really is, dunnit? Damned to hell and back! Well, why else did God desecrate His Own Altar with a bolt o' lightnin', if He hadn't got the Devil in him? 'Tis a thought, ent it? God is the Devil, an' the Devil is God. Or maybe there's no such thing as either… (*Trailing off and swivelling his head uncertainly.*) You still…there, Maggy? (*Pause.*) Well, are you?

MAGGY: (*Slight smile.*) Thought you had a sixth sense, luv?

ROB: Maggy!

(*MAGGY touches his forehead.*)

(*Oblivious.*) Last night, durin' the storm, I were under the window. Church bells were janglin' in the thunder. Then, even though I'm blind, I…*saw* the lightnin'! Saw it rip through the church roof, an' fire the altar. An' when I looked down into the street, the cobble stones were movin'!

(*JED re-appears with more tiles. MAGGY registers him but ROB is oblivious.*)

They were movin', I tell you! An' right below the window, the ground were openin' up like a great furrow between waves. Only lasted a moment. Then the furrow closed up again, grittin' its teeth on the heavin' cobble stones. Moment later, all I could see was a long, twisty crack, writhin' under our cottages, right the way up here to the graveyard. But I knew that deep in the veins o' the cliff, I knew the wound was still there, an' growin'. Growin'! Waitin' for the next bitch of a storm to rage into its heart, and tear our homes into the sea with it. (*Pause.*) Then God's Hook clawed my eyes out again. A black net swooshed down. The darkness took me. Now it's all muddied. An', worse – there's a surgin' in here. (*Indicating his forehead.*) Like millions of pebbles, rattlin' in the wake of a big wave…back into the deep.

(*ROB imitates the sounds of the pebbles surging in his head.*)

MAGGY: The fever's eatin' you up, luv.

ROB: (*Shaking his head.*) I saw the wound growin' in the cliff. And it were an omen, I tell you. The next storm'll have the Angel o' Death ridin' on her back, to blast us to Hell!

(*JED smiles contemptuously.*)

MAGGY: Not likely to be another storm like that for years.

ROB: Ent there? Not what that wind says.

(*ROB heads for the church. JED is about to restrain him but MAGGY shakes her head. JED steps aside. ROB goes.*)

MAGGY: (*After her husband has gone.*) No point. Each day, it's worse.

(*JED takes her hand. MAGGY looks at him for a moment, then gently removes her hand. Before he can speak, she goes. Pause.*

BETH HAXTON (sixty; chubby and cheery, although obviously in pain) puffs into view. BETH has a retching cough. She is followed by SANDRA WENLOCK who is angular, depressed and often silent. Between them, they are carrying a large carved angel that used to be one of the glories of the church roof.)

BETH: (*Calling over her shoulder.*) Vicar, look what we found under the rubble.

(*The VICAR appears.*)

VICAR: Is it badly damaged?

BETH: The angel's wing is broken, an' he's lost one o' his feet. (*Coughing.*) Where shall we put him?

VICAR: On that slab.

JED: (*Amused.*) Perfect place for a foot-loose angel with a bent flipper.

BETH: When he were above the altar, he were all golden and beautiful. Weren't he, Sandra? (*Pause.*) Well, don't just stand there ringin' yer hands, gal; say somethin'.

(*SANDRA continues to ring her hands.*)

VICAR: (*Examining the angel.*) The face is so charred, the lightning must have struck him on the head.

BETH: Looks more like one of them gargoyles now, don't he?

(*BETH laughs at her own joke, then coughs even harder. She is forced to sit on a tomb to recover from her coughing fit. JED pats her back but BETH shakes her head.*)

Thanks, Jed, but thumpin' only makes it worse.

(*Producing a bag of sweets.*) Anyone care for a bit of me home-made butterscotch?

(*Everyone but JED declines.*)

JED: Ta, Beth.

VICAR: Sure you're all right, Mrs Haxton?

BETH: Oh ay. Just feel a touch queasy, that's all. (*Belching.*) But butterscotch helps me burp.

VICAR: You still having your treatment up at the hospital, then?

BETH: Y'can say that again! But it's me rheumatics plagues me most. (*Painfully flexing her fingers and laughing.*) Should see them mittens I'm makin' for Maggy's little uns. They're more like slabs of tripe than gloves.
(*BETH burps.*)
(*Grinning.*) Beg pardon. Better than up-chuckin', though, ent it?
(*BETH laughs and coughs.*)
(*To SANDRA.*) Well, laugh, gal. Won't kill you.
(*SANDRA shakes her head.*)
If you wring them hands any harder, they'll fall off.
(*BETH has another laughing-coughing fit.*)

VICAR: (*Concerned.*) Let me take you home, Mrs Haxton.

BETH: (*Moving back towards the church.*) I'm better off here helpin', thanks, Vicar. (*Laughing and pointing at ROB who is still working by the church.*) 'Sides, Pink-Bloomers Rob there looks like he can do with some help.
(*BETH goes out laughing.*)

VICAR: Her treatment hasn't stopped it spreading, then?

SANDRA: 'Fraid not.

JED: Poor cow.
(*Off, BETH says something that is inaudible, then laughs.*)

SANDRA: How can she keep on laughin' like that, when everything's so hopeless?
(*ROB returns with another huge beam.*)

ROB: Beth reckons we've only got to clear a bit more from around the main entrance, then we can get the main door open.
(*ROB throws down his beam and goes off.*)

VICAR: Right, let's help Mrs Haxton. Then we can go inside and give thanks that the damage isn't worse.
(*JED bars his way.*)

JED: You're not seriously thinkin' of holdin' a service in that charnel house, are you?

111

VICAR: It'll be quite safe at this end by the font. Only round the altar that it's not…

(*There is a fierce gust of wind.*)

JED: 'Safe'? One pious word resonating inside that door, an' a dozen tiles'll come crashin' down round yer halo.

(*Sound of falling tiles.*)

VICAR: Mm… you may have a point.

JED: (*Grabbing the VICAR's sleeve.*) So why don't you stop pretendin', Vicar, and admit it?

VICAR: (*Rearranging his cassock.*) Admit what?

JED: Admit that your god-game's over! It's our cottages we're worried about, not that obsolete pile of stones.

(*MAGGY returns with tiles and rubble in a wheel-barrow. JED indicates MAGGY and SANDRA to the VICAR.*)

If you don't believe me, look at the despair in their eyes.

MAGGY: Just 'cause things've been a bit rough lately, don't mean we're despairin'.

JED: 'Bit rough'? This cliff an' everything on it could go crashin' down into the sea, and you call that just 'a bit rough'?

SANDRA: (*Near to tears.*) God won't let it happen, will He, Vicar?

VICAR: Sandra, God is not responsible…

JED: 'Not responsible'? – For an Act of God? (*To SANDRA.*) That's what the insurance people'll call it.

(*SANDRA sobs and rushes back to the church. MAGGY follows her, trying to comfort her.*)

VICAR: (*Calling after her.*) Sandra, please don't upset yourself.

MAGGY: (*As she disappears.*) 'S'alright, I'll cheer her up.

VICAR: You needn't have done that, Jed.

JED: Told you there was nuthin' left for you here, didn't I? So why don't you just lift up yer raven's skirts, an' flap back to East Haven where you belong?

VICAR: Stop poking me.

JED: They've a proper church there, with a whole roof on, and a nice, prosperous congregation underneath it. I understand they can even afford to believe in the resurrection in East Haven.

(*BETH appears with more debris, followed by ROB who is shouldering another huge beam.*)

BETH: Now you've said more'n enough, Jed Thomas. That be a Man of God you're blasphemin' at.

ROB: (*Throwing down his beam.*) Ay, damned we may be, but there's no need for you to be insultin'.

JED: (*Laughing.*) 'Blasphemin''? 'Damned'? My friends, my friends; what's his so-called 'saviour' ever done for either of you?

VICAR: Mr Thomas, I suggest you go home before you say...

JED: (*Interrupting.*) Well, what *has* his saviour done for any of you in this shitty village?

VICAR: Go home, Mr Thomas.

JED: If your saviour boy's not blessed him with blindness... (*Indicating BETH.*) ...he's given her cancer!

BETH: (*Recovering from another coughing fit.*) How can you say such things?

JED: 'Cause I have to say 'em! Well, someone's got to say somethin'! – if this village is ever goin' to drag itself into the twenty-first century.

ROB: Oh don't start all that again.

BETH: (*Following ROB off.*) Ay, someone's got to make 'emselves useful.

VICAR: Yes, Mr Thomas, if you insist on driving us all crazy, the least you can do is help us stack this lot outside the graveyard. Then we can begin to sort everything out.

JED: You mean we've now got to take everythin' outside the graveyard?

VICAR: We can't leave the beams and all this rubble propped up against Mrs Rigby's gravestone, can we? So you can start by moving that barrow load, please.
(*The VICAR follows his own advice and carries the various boxes of rubble off to the other side. Grumbling JED picks up the wheelbarrow, and kicks a beam in passing.*)

JED: (*Shouting.*) Why don't we just chuck all these beams over the cliff, Vicar, an' be done with it? Then come the next storm, our cottages'll have somethin' holy to land on.

(*JED is going out with his load when SANDRA comes in with more debris.*)

SANDRA: (*Tearfully to JED.*) If my Andrew were here, he'd stop you sayin' all them dreadful things to the Vicar.

JED: But 'your Andrew' isn't here, Sandra. He's had the sense to give up on all this church baloney.

SANDRA: (*Covering her ears.*) I don't want to hear…

JED: (*Cutting.*) Naturally; because the only reason 'your Andrew' ever went to church was…

SANDRA: (*Overriding him.*) I don't want to hear it, I tell you!

JED: (*Smiling.*) Yes, and in that regard, you're just like everyone else.

(*The VICAR returns as JED goes out with his load.*)

VICAR: (*Comforting SANDRA.*) He doesn't know what he's talking about, Sandra, believe me.

JED: (*Off.*) You can't take the truth about yourselves, can you?

VICAR: (*Calling back.*) Can anyone, Mr Thomas? Even you? (*BETH comes in with more debris.*)

BETH: 'Least of all him. He's got a bolt loose. (*JED comes charging back with his barrow.*)

JED: Rousseau's right: 'Man is born free but everywhere he's in chains'!

VICAR: (*Laughing.*) Mrs Haxton's right: constant exposure to the State School system has obviously driven you insane. (*MAGGY comes in, laughing, and dumps her load on JED's barrow. The VICAR wheels the barrow out.*)

JED: Only doomed slaves chortle at their chains. Still, what else can you expect so long as that rich bitch on the hill continues to shackle you to her fields year in and year out?

BETH: Leave Mrs Allbright out o' this.

MAGGY: Ay, she's a kind-hearted…

JED: …Patronisin', predatory cow!…

BETH: Oh give over, Jed.

JED: …Who not only owns every strip of land as far as the eye can see, but also she owns every godforsaken cottage in Seafall, too. So every bite you eat, every room you live in, an' all yer workin' hours belong to that bitch, Mrs 'Kind-Hearted' Allbright!

BETH: I don't care what you say; she's a darn good employer.

SANDRA: Yes, you're never fair, Jed.

JED: Will she be fair to you when the next storm rips your houses apart?

(*ROB lumbers in with another beam.*)

ROB: (*His pipe clenched between his teeth.*) Now you listen here, Jed Thomas. If you say one more thing that I don't like – an' anythin' you say, I *won't* like – I'm goin' to tear you limb from limb, right!

JED: Can't you understand? Come the next bastard storm, you'll all have no roofs over yer heads. But Mrs All-Bitch-Bright will! So you've got to force her to give you some of her land, an' now while there's time. She can afford to give it 'cause she's got thousands of acres of it. Then you can build yourselves new homes on it, an' we can…well, we farm the land as a collective.

BETH: (*Laughing.*) 'As a collective'?

MAGGY: Yes, that kind of nonsense went out years ago.

BETH: (*Nodding.*) He's gone right off his chump this time.

JED: I'm sorry but I don't understand what the hell you're all waitin' for!

(*The VICAR re-appears with the barrow.*)

VICAR: (*Beaming.*) A moment of sanity, perhaps?

JED: You supercilious, pontificatin' dog-collar!

VICAR: At least I'm not an antediluvian-do-it-yourself-Marxist-fantasist!

(*Everyone laughs at JED.*)

JED: I give up on the lot of you!

VICAR: Whose contribution to the salvation of this village seems to consist entirely of stentorian envy and dialectical gibberish.

BETH: (*Mystified by the VICAR's words but obviously pleased.*) That's it, you tell him, Vicar, you tell him.

JED: (*Slyly, to the VICAR.*) I'm glad we both agree that Seafall is in imminent need of 'salvation'.

VICAR: (*Disconcerted.*) That's not what I meant.

JED: So I'm sure these good folk would like to hear your solution for saving their cottages. (*Pause.*) Well, don't be modest, Monsignor; we're all ears. Pray do expound.
(*There is a sudden violent gust of wind. The others who have been laughing at JED, now turn expectant eyes on the VICAR who smiles self-consciously.*)
(*Indicating the wind.*) An' swiftish, Vicar, before we all blown into the sea.

VICAR: Well...

ROB: Yes?
(*Another fierce gust.*)

VICAR: You know my solution. You should go and live in a ...well, a less dangerous location.

BETH: Seafall's our home, Vicar!

MAGGY: Ay, our fathers lived here.

ROB: An' our forefathers.

SANDRA: We belong here, Vicar.
(*The wind increases in intensity.*)

VICAR: Then you'll just have to try and...well, look on the bright side of things, won't you?

JED: (*Grinning.*) Is there one?

VICAR: You know very well that last night's was a freak storm. There won't be another like it for years.
(*The wind rages.*)

ROB: Don't sound like that to me. Only thing'll save us now's a bloody miracle!

JED: So why don't you creak down on yer benders an' pray for one? An' see where that'll get you.

BETH: Ay, why *don't* we pray for one?

JED: I'm only jokin'!

BETH: I'm not.

JED: (*Laughing.*) Nothing's ever that bad.

BETH: What's wrong with prayin'? Well, what *is* wrong with prayin', Vicar?

VICAR: (*Hesitant.*) Well, nothing, Mrs Haxton...

SANDRA: A miracle at least would make a change.

VICAR: This is the twenty-first century, Sandra, so recently there's been a shortage in the miracle department.

(*The wind is now continuous.*)

BETH: What are we waiting for? No point standin' an'
freezin', when we can just as easy kneel down an' pray.

JED: (*In disbelief.*) Kneel out here?

BETH: Well, we can't pray inside the church, can we? In
any other age of the world, folk'd pray anywhere if their
fear an' need were great enough. I only have to take a
peak at that crack runnin' under my house to know how
scared I am. (*To the others as she shouts above the wind.*) And
if you're all too proud to join me, I'll pray on me
lonesome.

(*BETH kneels.*)

MAGGY: (*To the VICAR.*) We might as well give it a go,
Vicar.

(*MAGGY kneels.*)

JED: I don't believe this! You can't have an open-air prayer
meeting.

ROB: I'm game, Beth, if you are.

(*ROB kneels.*)

SANDRA: Yes, what've we got to lose?

(*SANDRA kneels.*)

JED: I don't believe that you're all going to...

VICAR: (*Interrupting.*) That's your problem. You don't
believe in anything. Not even in yourself. (*He kneels.*)
Why don't you join us, Jed, and pray for some belief?

ROB: Ay, give yer pride a rest for once, Thomas.

JED: You'll never get me down on my benders!

(*The wind howls around them.*)

BETH: For God's sake, Vicar, just say one of yer prayers for
help!

VICAR: But the chance of a miracle...

ROB: (*Cutting him.*) We know, so pray!

(*Pause.*)

SANDRA: Please!

MAGGY: Come on, Vicar.

BETH: Ay, 'cos this ground's settin' off me rheumatics
some'at chronic.

ROB: (*As the sky darkens.*) An' another storm's comin'!

VICAR: All right, I'll try.

(*JED moves away in disgust, and stares out to sea.*)

JED: Talk about embarrassin'. Not to mention pathetic.

VICAR: (*Praying above the wind.*) Almighty God, You know only too well the tragic consequences of another storm on this beleaguered village. So we humbly beseech You to take pity on these, Your loving servants...

ROB: No, Lord, we BEG You to be merciful! I can bear bein' blind – just! – but, for Christ sake, remove Your Curse from us, Lord, and from this godforsaken place!

VICAR: Rob, Seafall is not damned!

JED: Jesus, it's enough to make you heave.

BETH: (*Now shouting above the wind.*) Don't strike Jed Thomas down, Lord. He ent worth the consideration. Besides, I don't think the cliff'll stand up to another bolt of lightnin'. But seriously, Lord, give us back the seasons like we used to have 'em.

MAGGY: An' no more storms!

SANDRA: Or we'll lose our homes.

BETH: Jus' give us a glimpse of spring sun shine, Lord.

ROB: Free us from the lashin' wind!

MAGGY: (*Close to ROB.*) Take away the darkness, Lord.

JED: How can you pray to the elements? 'Cause that's exactly what you're doin'.

BETH: Lord, anything's possible. Anythin'! If only You will it so!

MAGGY: You can save us, Lord, if You want to.

VICAR: Help them, Lord. Hear our prayer.

THE VILLAGERS: (*Except JED.*) Hear us, Lord; help us!

(*Their cries are almost drowned by the howling wind.*)

ROB: GIVE US A SIGN, LORD, A SIGN!

(*After a moment, the wind dies down a little.*)

JED: There's no point in waitin', folks. This is the twenty-first century, remember. So nothing miraculous is goin' to happen.

(*The wind dies down even more, then drops completely.*)

(*Laughing.*) Well, you've had your 'sign'. An' it's all you're likely to get. So now what?

(*Still laughing, JED turns away from the VILLAGERS –
only to come face to face with a bearded STRANGER in his
mid-thirties, who has materialised from the direction of the
church.*

*The STRANGER has a weather-beaten, charismatic face.
His clothes have also seen better days. He is carrying an old
rucksack.*

*The VILLAGERS look up in surprise, because not only has
the wind dropped but the first ray of spring sunshine has
broken through the cloud bank.*

*Gradually the sun illuminates the graveyard, gilding the tombs.
The VILLAGERS are dumbfounded. Even JED looks
stunned.*)

STRANGER: (*Smiling.*) Thank Heaven for that.

BETH: (*Laughing.*) Don't worry, Stranger, we will.

(*The STRANGER moves further into the graveyard. He has
mischievous eyes.*)

STRANGER: Beginning to think it'd never come out today.

ROB: (*Standing.*) What?

MAGGY: (*Joining him.*) The sun, sweetheart. The sun.

ROB: (*To the STRANGER.*) Who are you?

STRANGER: (*Indicating BETH who is still on her knees.*)
Sorry if I'm disturbing your prayer meeting but I do
believe I'm vaguely lost.

VICAR: Anyone who brings the sun on his shoulder has no
need to be sorry. About anything.

ROB: (*To the STRANGER.*) Who are you?

STRANGER: (*Indicating the sun.*) 'Fraid our fortuitous
arrival is purely a coincidence. (*Smiling.*) Unfortunately.

BETH: (*Still kneeling.*) Is it?

JED: (*Recovering his poise.*) 'Course it is!

(*The VICAR shivers.*)

SANDRA: Someone step over yer grave, Vicar?

(*The VICAR shakes his head in disbelief.*)

VICAR: Can't believe it.

STRANGER: What?

VICAR: (*Staring at the STRANGER.*) Surely we…?

STRANGER: What?

VICAR: I am right. It was you…

STRANGER: Coincidence.

VICAR: If you say so.

STRANGER: I do.

VICAR: Oh...listen.

ROB: To what?

VICAR: Surely you can hear them, Rob?

JED: Hear what?

VICAR: The birds.

SANDRA: First time I noticed 'em this year.

MAGGY: And the wind's completely dropped.

ROB: (*Touching his own face.*) I can feel the sun.

BETH: (*Indicating the bird song.*) So can they.

VICAR: Wonderful, it's just wonderful. (*Pause.*) Thank you, Lord.

(*BETH winces and buckles to her knees. The STRANGER and JED move to help her.*)

JED: Steady, Ma, steady.

BETH: 'S'nuthin'. Just me screwmatics. All that praying's locked me knees up tighter'n a piggy-bank.

STRANGER: Here, put your weight on my arm. Now sit down and take it easy.

BETH: Thank you. (*Puzzled as she clasps his hand.*) Strange.

MAGGY: What is?

BETH: Hold my hand tighter, will you, sir?

STRANGER: What?

BETH: No, tighter than that.

VICAR: Do you know this man, Mrs Haxton?

BETH: (*To the STRANGER.*) Now clench me fingers, sir, an' squeeze 'em real hard.

STRANGER: (*Concerned as he squeezes her hand.*) If I squeeze 'em any harder, I'll cut off your circulation altogether.

VICAR: Mrs Haxton, a graveyard's hardly the place for...

BETH: (*Overriding him.*) No doubt about it.

ROB: What's going on?

BETH: I definitely feel...a bit better.

STRANGER: I didn't realise you were feeling ill.

(*Pause.*)

BETH: Didn't you? (*After another pause.*) You know, sir, don't you?

STRANGER: (*Laughing.*) No.

BETH: The moment you helped me up, the awful nausea I always have, well, it started to go.

STRANGER: I'm glad you're feeling better. It's incredible what a burst of sunshine can do, isn't it?

BETH: (*Looking him in the eyes.*) All right, sir. If that's the way you want it.

JED: Vicar, do you know what she's on about?
(*The VICAR shakes his head.*)

ROB: I'm always in the dark but this is ridiculous.

STRANGER: (*Laughing.*) You can say that again.

BETH: No use you laughin' it off, sir. I know what I feel. So if you fancy a bite of dinner, mine's the first cottage in the village. The one with the pink door.
(*BETH turns to go.*)

SANDRA: (*Mystified.*) So…are you're all right, Beth?

BETH: I'm much better'n I was.
(*BETH seizes the STRANGER's hand.*)
Sorry! Just can't help meself.

STRANGER: (*Amused.*) So I see.

BETH: (*Releasing his hand.*) No doubt about it. Well, don't forget to come over, sir. There's turnip wine to whet yer whistle for starters, an' jam roly-poly for arters.
(*BETH winks and goes.*)

MAGGY: What, in God's name, has come over her?

ROB: (*To the STRANGER.*) Yes, who are you?

VICAR: Yes, Mr er…?

STRANGER: Just an odd-jobber passing through. (*Indicating the beams from the church roof.*) Storm must've been terrible.

JED: Were you in the vicinity?

STRANGER: No.

ROB: Then how'd you know that there's been in a storm?

STRANGER: (*Pointing to the church.*) What else could've ripped your church roof off? 'Cept a whirlwind.
(*Mischievously.*) Or God's Wrath.
(*The STRANGER examines the fallen angel.*)
I'll try and carve a new face for your angel if you like. I enjoy restoring things. Then I could doctor his wing, stick the other one back on, and give him a new foot. If

you like my work, I could even repair your church roof. Oh you don't need to worry about paying me. (*Gesturing towards BETH's cottage.*) If Mrs er...will see I'm fed and watered, I'll be more than content. So what d'you say? (*They stare at him.*)

VICAR: Well, that's very generous of you, Mr er...?

STRANGER: (*Interrupting with a smile.*) Think about it. I'll be over at Mrs er... (*Waving.*) And a very good morning to you. (*Indicating the sun.*) And it really *is* now, isn't it? (*Before they can respond, the STRANGER has gone.*)

JED: (*Watching him go.*) I wonder what his game is?

ROB: Maybe he don't have one. (*Grinning.*) Then what will you do?

JED: You know him from somewhere, Vicar, don't you?

VICAR: (*Going off.*) For a moment I thought there was something familiar about him but I'm obviously mistaken.

JED: (*Following him.*) What about the clearing-up? (*ROB loads up the wheelbarrow with MAGGY.*)

ROB: Seems they've left it all to us.

MAGGY: (*Guiding him in the direction of the church wall.*) It is a bit odd, though, ent it?

ROB: What is?

(*SANDRA and MAGGY exchange looks, then MAGGY and ROB go off – leaving SANDRA alone. For a moment it seems as if SANDRA is going to cry again. Instead she crosses herself and goes back towards the church...leaving the empty graveyard which is now filled with bird-song in dazzling sunshine.*)

Scene 2

Seafall Beach; the base of the fissured cliff.

There is the lazy hiss of untroubled waves as they lap around...the audience. And the intermittent cry of gulls.

The STRANGER (from now on known as JOE) sits astride an up-turned rowing boat, his bare feet in the sand. With a chisel, JOE is putting the finishing touches to the angel's wing. He pauses to mop his brow.

It is surprisingly hot for early April.

JOE stares out to sea.

ROB limps into view, leaning heavily on a walking stick. His blindness seems more apparent than usual. SIMON (the old fisherman of the village) accompanies him. They are arguing.

JOE is hypnotised by the sea so he does not react to their argument.

ROB: Couldn't have! 'S'like the Vicar said; it's just a coincidence.

SIMON: That's what I thought first off.
    (*ROB stumbles. SIMON supports him.*)

ROB: God damn these stones! They're nearly as treacherous as our schoolteacher.

SIMON: Now don't try'n change the subject. Y'know as well as I do that; I caught more lobsters, crabs an' crayfish past couple of days than I done all last year.
    (*ROB points his stick vaguely in JOE's direction.*)

ROB: You...still there, Joe?

JOE: (*Coming out of his reverie.*) Most of me. Why?

ROB: You tell Simon, then.

JOE: Tell him what?

ROB: You're comin' here, and the changes in weather an' that, well, they are a coincidence – like I say they are.

JOE: (*Laughing and returning to his carving.*) 'Course they are.

SIMON: C'mon, friend, ever since you came to Seafall, we've had scarce a breath of wind, an' endless sunshine days. An' in these parts it's just plain unnatural at this time of the year.

ROB: Or any other.

SIMON: Then there's the flowers. God in Heaven, here we are, just turned April, an' the daffodils are out. Scarce a fortnight ago their buds were shut tight as a mackerel's arse. There's coltsfoot glistenin' on the clifftop, an' cross wort, green hellebore an' shepherd's purse. Even seen a meadow speckled with Lent lilies yester-eve. An' I never knowed them to come out 'till the backside of May. So how'd you explain that?

JOE: (*Laughing.*) I can't. But I'm very glad I'm here to see them.

SIMON: You tryin' to tell me that my catches, an' this broilin' heat, an' the plants sproutin' like billy-o, have nuthin' to do with you comin' here?

JOE: (*Still smiling.*) 'Course they haven't.

ROB: What did I tell you, Simon?

SIMON: (*To JOE.*) They prayed for you to come, y'know.

ROB: Weren't prayin' for him!

SIMON: Ay, but you prayed. Beth told me. You lot were down on yer benders pleadin' for a miracle. (*To JOE.*) Then you appeared in the graveyard.

ROB: Ent denyin' that. But you ent the miracle, Joe. Are you?

JOE: Certainly not. Only thing miraculous about me is how I've managed to survive so long, doing so little. But seriously... (*Holding up the carved angel for their inspection.*) ...what d'you think? Have I patched him up all right? Is he good enough to grace your church roof?

(*SIMON examines the angel. ROB tries to sit on the edge of the upturned boat but loses his balance. JOE steadies ROB and helps him to sit down safely. Then ROB shrugs JOE away.*)

ROB: I hate bein' helped! (*Instantly contrite.*) Sorry, Joe. Just wish I could see what you've done with the angel.

SIMON: (*About the angel.*) Not bad at all.

JOE: Thank you.

SIMON: 'Fact I ent seen craft like it since me old Dad carved them side pews forty odd year ago. (*Passing the angel to ROB.*) Here, run yer fingers over his wings.

ROB: Mmm...feathers are as good as new.

JOE: Glad they meet with your approval.

(*Suddenly SIMON reaches out and takes JOE's hand and examines it.*)

What's the matter, Simon?

SIMON: My Dad had real carpenter's hands.

JOE: (*Smiling.*) I know. My calluses are new. (*Shrugging.*) But then I'm a very half-hearted carpenter. Though on good days, when I'm actually carving, a kind of fever seems to course through me. Then my work shows flare. But mostly I find myself just sitting. Watching the waves as they cream around the rocks. Then an oyster-catcher dives. (*Pointing.*) Like so! A tern shoots after him into the spray. Sun dazzles the beach. And my mind's dazzled, too. It's as if all this is merely…a shimmering mirage. Y'know, the sand here is almost as bright as in the Sinai Desert.

ROB: (*Lighting his pipe.*) That your idea of a sermon?

SIMON: More like a parable.

JOE: (*Laughing.*) It wasn't meant to be either. Just trying to explain why I never seem to achieve anything. (*Producing a wine bottle from behind the boat.*) Care for a swig?

ROB: What is it?

JOE: Mrs Haxton's turnip wine. (*Drinking and belching.*) Oh it's brimful of acid and gives you the gripes, but strangers can't be choosers. She's a magnificent cook, though. 'Specially her toad in the hole and her mussel pasties.

(*JOE passes SIMON the bottle. The old fisherman sits cross-legged on the beach and drinks*)

SIMON: You don't have to tell me. 'Fact, once, after I woofed down a couple of her pasties, I told her straight out that she should wed me. An' for a few hours we were as good as plighted. Then when the turnip wine wore off, we realised we'd be hopeless together. So we lay back an' laughed ourselves helpless. Don't look so grim, Rob. I bet if you asked our friend here nice, he might give you your sight back. Well, he's made our Beth better.

(*SIMON passes the bottle to ROB. Then SIMON takes out his snuff box.*)

ROB: Beth's not really better, an' deep down she knows she ent!

JOE: I'm sure you're right. Only thing I did was bruise her poor old fingers in the graveyard. (*Watching ROB massage his ankle.*) Does that hurt a lot?

ROB: A mite.

JOE: Someone ought to fix those steps down to the beach.

SIMON: (*After sneezing on his snuff.*) How'd you know he did it on the steps?

JOE: I didn't. But I almost turned my ankle on 'em yesterday. (*Reaching for the bottle.*) Rob, d'you mind if I...?
(*ROB hands him the bottle. JOE drinks. SIMON watches him.*)
Mmm...the savour of wine on your tongue – even turnip wine – combined with the salt tang of sea in your nostrils, must be amongst the most sensuous combinations this side of Paradise.

ROB: You never said where you come from.

JOE: Just passing through. But you people continue to intrigue me. Well, how can you bear to live on the edge of a crumbling cliff? Especially as you say the cliff's going to give way under your houses any day now, and thunder into the sea?
(*BETH appears, with a bag of sweets.*)

BETH: Want one?
(*Only JOE accepts.*)

JOE: Thank you, Mrs H. These home-made, too?

BETH: Ay, but don't worry about the green chewy-bit in the middle. 'S'only arsenic. (*Laughing and hugging JOE.*) You've made me so happy.

SIMON: Hey, steady on, Beth.

JOE: (*Struggling to free himself from BETH's ample embrace.*) Yes, do we really have to go through this cuddling routine again?
(*Laughing BETH reluctantly releases him.*)

BETH: Sorry. 'S'lovely, though...gettin' me old hands on a proper man. 'Specially now I've got some life back in me fingers.

JOE: You're an outrageous flirt, Mrs H.

BETH: True, but that's only 'cause you've made me feel so much better. 'Fact I believe you're actually curin' me.

JOE: Get away with you.

SIMON: (*To ROB, in response to BETH's assertion.*) What did I tell you?

ROB: How can he cure you, Beth, when even the doctors don't know how to cure...?

JOE: (*Interrupting.*) Exactly.

BETH: (*Squeezing JOE's shoulder.*) What you're doin' for me is little short of miraculous, I tell you!

JOE: If it's 'miraculous', it definitely rules me out. Oh I'm not saying that I wouldn't like to work miracles. Who wouldn't?

(*JED appears with MAGGY.*)

MAGGY: Wondered where you lot had got to.

JOE: I bet even Jed would agree with me.

JED: What?

JOE: I was saying there are times in our lives when we'd give anything to possess supernatural powers.

JED: I'd never go that far.

JOE: (*Working on the angel with his chisel.*) But unfortunately I'm merely a common-or-garden wine-bibber who's just passing through. And not even doing that particularly well.

SIMON: You don't believe that.

JOE: 'Course I do. (*His chisel slips.*) Now look what you've made me! I've shaved the tip of his wing off.

MAGGY: Oh no.

JOE: Oh yes!

BETH: Can't you glue it back on?

JOE: For pete's sake! Look...would you all mind leaving me on my tod for a bit? Before I chop his head off as well.

SIMON: You're here for a purpose, ent you?

JED: Yes; to make fools out of you lot.

MAGGY: (*To JOE.*) Will it help if I hold the angel while you glue him?

JOE: The only help I need at the moment is for you all to leave me in peace! (*Opening a tube of wood glue.*) All right?

ROB: That's it, Joe, you tell 'em.

(*BETH laughs and pops another sweet into her mouth.*)

JED: (*To BETH.*) You can go on laughing 'till kingdom come. But it still doesn't alter the facts. An' the central fact is our Bearded Wonder here isn't curin' you.

BETH: He is!

JOE: Oh give it a rest, Mrs H. Oh Jesus! Now I've got glue all over his feathers.

ROB: (*Cleaning his pipe.*) Ay, Beth, don't start all that 'miraculous' nonsense again.

BETH: (*Oblivious.*) Lord save us! If only you had a bit of faith, Rob Bulford, he'd give you your sight back an' all. (*Turning on JOE.*) Well, don't just sit there sloppin' glue all over yerself. Do some'at for the poor sod!

JOE: (*Laughing.*) Like what?

MAGGY: (*To JOE, about the angel's wing.*) You've glued that bit on crooked.

(*JOE throws down his tube of glue.*)

JOE: All right, all right; if this is the way you want to play it.

SIMON: (*Triumphantly wiping his snuff-stained fingers down his shirt front.*) No, you're the one that's playing games, Joe. 'Cause *you're* testin' us, right?

JOE: Oi veh!

(*JOE stands, furiously wiping the glue off his hands with a rag. Then he throws the rag down.*)

(*Smiling and nodding.*) But I suppose it serves me right for spending forty days in the wilderness.

ROB: You spent forty days in the Wilderness?

JOE: (*Beaming.*) Thirty-eight and a half actually. On an Israeli package tour. But I'm sure little blemishes like that won't spoil my mythical prospects.

JED: (*Frenziedly searching for his matches as his cigarette has gone out.*) Now don't you start encouraging 'em, for God's sake.

BETH: Perhaps it were for 'God's sake' that he were sent here.

JOE: Beth, you really are incredible. I shouldn't tell you this but...you are the double of my mother. And my mother's so religious, she insists she's been a virgin all her life. (*JOE is now the only one who is standing, save for JED. The others are literally sitting at his feet.*)

JED: Oh don't sit there gawpin' at him!

MAGGY: (*To JOE.*) Did your mother truly say she's been...a life-long virgin?

JOE: Still does. But I got my own back on her when I was twelve. What's more, in the church... (*Smiling apologetically.*) ...Sorry; temple.

JED: (*To the others.*) Can't you see he's takin' the piss out of you?

ROB: Why don't you shut up, teacher, and listen? You might learn somethin'.

JED: He's deliberately bein' blasphemous.

BETH: Be quiet, will you? (*To JOE.*) So what happened to you in the temple when you were twelve?

JOE: Not a lot. The Vicar's sermon was so boring, suddenly I found myself on my feet interrupting him in full flow. I couldn't take him wheezing on about Job and his boils any longer.

(*JED laughs. The others regard JED with contempt.*)

So I told the old boy to sit down and play with his crosier. Then I proceeded to deliver an impromptu sermon of my own on the habitually hypnotic subject of Sunday schools.

JED: (*Laughing.*) Stop, you'll give me a stitch, Joe. Mind, you are doing my atheism a power of good.

JOE: (*Winking at JED.*) Wait, it gets better.

SIMON: This all true, Joe?

JOE: Of course. And I ended my sermon by telling the Vicar and all the parents that they should attend Sunday school themselves.

BETH: Why?

JOE: So they could be taught a few home-truths by us kids for a change. The congregation was so titillated by my divine cheek that they gave me a standing ovation. (*Indicating his head.*) Hence this permanent halo. Which, unfortunately, is only visible when the sun is due west. (*Pause.*)

BETH: Don't move, Master!

JOE: Why are you all staring? (*As they continue to stare.*) That was a joke about my halo! And my mother's on-going virginity. And the Sermon on the Mount... (*Quickly.*) I mean, in the temple...church! Look, I don't even believe in God. Or what I've just done would be – like Jed said – an act of deliberate blasphemy.

JED: Right.

(*The others ignore JED, their eyes still fixed on JOE.*)

JOE: What I'm trying to say is; I have no power beyond spewing out a few outrageous words and patching up the odd angel.

(*JOE turns away from them. JED grins, folding his arms, waiting. BETH goes to JOE and takes his hands.*)

BETH: Don't worry, Master. Even doubters like Rob there are beginnin' to believe.

JOE: (*Breaking away.*) But there's nothing in me to believe in!

BETH: You're wrong. In my heart I know that if you will it so, Rob will regain his sight.

SIMON: Give the man his sight back, Joe. Rob's suffered long enough, surely?

JED: Haven't we all?

JOE: Yes, why do you all refuse to understand? I've about as much chance of restoring Rob's sight as I have of...I don't know...of changing the direction of that cloud. (*Mock-challenging the cloud in question.*) Well, go on, cloud. BLOT OUT THE SUN!

(*Pause.*)

See. No response. Anymore than I can force the incoming tide to retreat. I'm not saying that it isn't possible to do these things. 'Fact I'm sure we have the power to control the elements latent inside us. But we don't know how to tap that power yet, let alone exploit it. So please don't waste your time having visions of folk walking on the water, or raising the dead, or hurling their minds to the far side of the galaxy. That's all in an inconceivable future. Godamnit, we still don't utilise more than a fifth of our available brain cells, never mind having the power to reverse the direction of a cloud by an act of will. (*Pause.*) Well, one thing's certain; *I* haven't broken through my mind-barrier. I can't make fantasies into reality. To do so would require inordinate genius. And above all, I would need to possess monumental faith in order to unleash any miraculous force, even if such a force is latent inside us. And I have so little knowledge of myself. I don't know what I'm on the earth for. Or whether I'm here for anything at all. Anyway...perhaps we are all just...dreaming each other. (*Grinning at JED.*) Or should I say – nightmaring? (*Shaking his head at BETH.*) Don't stare at me, Beth, with those great eyes. Look, I can't be held responsible for your pain, Maggy. And I certainly can't answer your prayers, Rob. So please be sensible, all of you. Go home and forget me. As soon as I've finished the angel, I'll pack my things and disappear. (*Quickly.*) But not literally!

(*BETH and SIMON look up at the sky.*)

No use beseeching Heaven, my friends. There's no one up there to help you, either.

(*ROB grabs JOE's arm.*)

What are you doing?

ROB: Try! 'Least you can try to give me back my sight.

JOE: I can't, Rob.

ROB: How'd you know 'till you try?!

JOE: If I could I would but... I've no more chance of restoring your sight than I have of...calling a bolt of lightning out of the sky to strike some faith into me!

BETH: You've got the Lord's Power streamin' from you.

JOE: Beth!

BETH: Put spittle on yer fingers, then place yer fingers on his eyes, an' on the instant Rob will see again.

JOE: (*Laughing.*) Put spittle on my fingers? That's just another Jesus myth.

ROB: What've you got to lose?

JOE: Rob, how many times do I...?

ROB: (*Cutting.*) How many times do I have to beg you to help me? You said that you'd cure me if you could. If you don't try, we'll never know, will we? Or don't you want to cure me?

JOE: At this moment, believe me, there's nothing more I want in the world.

MAGGY: Then cure him.

ROB: Please try.

JOE: All right, all right. Anything to end this. But it won't work. And in your hearts, you know it.

(*JOE wets his fingertips, then he places his fingers on ROB's eyes.*)

There. (*Shrugging.*) That's it.

(*Long pause. Then JOE hugs ROB.*)

You still can't see, can you? Takes a lot more than spittle to make a miracle.

(*Pause.*)

ROB: Gone cold, ent it?

JED: Only a cloud passing over the sun.

(*The others shake their heads and continue to look up. Then BETH kneels and takes JOE's hand.*)

JOE: (*Laughing but alarmed.*) That's a different cloud, Beth!

BETH: It's the same one, Master.

JOE: (*Shaking his head.*) I pointed to that long fluffy one over there.

SIMON: Nay, you pointed at that great black bugger that's now coverin' the sun.

JOE: It was that fluffy one, I tell you!

MAGGY: No.

JOE: Yes well... I think I'd better make tracks...

(*As JOE moves away, there is a searing flash of lightning that knocks ROB's stick out of his hand. Then ROB crumples to the ground, and lies still.*

Stunned, the OTHERS stare helplessly at ROB's motionless body.)

JED: Jesus God!

(*MAGGY recovers sufficiently to tend her husband.*)

MAGGY: Sweetheart...

JOE: (*Laughing in anger.*) I suppose now you're going to accuse me of trying to kill the poor bastard?

JED: Don't be absurd. (*To the others.*) For God's sake, pull yourselves together an' help me get Rob up to Doctor Williams before the heavens really go berserk.

(*MAGGY listens to ROB's heart-beat.*)

MAGGY: Just a minute, Jed. He's goin' to be all right!

SIMON: He can't be, Maggy.

BETH: Yes, the lightnin' hit him full on.

JOE: It hit his stick actually. (*Taking hold of ROB's wrist.*) Good God, his pulse is almost normal.

JED: (*To the others who are crowding round.*) Give him some air, for pity's sake.

MAGGY: He's comin' round!

SIMON: It's a miracle!

JOE: It's not a miracle. We just live in a ridiculous climate.

BETH: (*Looking at JOE.*) Question is, who's responsible for the climate?

JOE: Look, if you have a freak heat-wave at the beginning of April, sooner or later it's bound to culminate in a freak thunder-storm.

MAGGY: (*To ROB.*) Now don't try'n sit up, luv.

JED: Yes, steady, man, steady.

JOE: (*To MAGGY.*) Shouldn't someone fetch a doctor?

SIMON: Still looks pretty stunned, don't he?

JED: Wouldn't you be?

ROB: (*Coming round.*) Don't need a doctor.

MAGGY: You all right, sweetheart?

ROB: (*Sitting up.*) I...think I am.

BETH: (*Crossing herself.*) The Lord be praised!
(*ROB seizes JOE's wrist.*)

ROB: I am! I'm all right! I am, Joe.

JOE: (*Laughing.*) You've still got a grip like a bull terrier.
(*Unsettled.*) What's the matter?

MAGGY: (*About ROB, to JOE.*) He can...SEE you. Can't you, luv?

JED: Oh c'mon, Maggy...

MAGGY: It's the first time for two whole years that he can see!

JOE: Maggy!

ROB: No! She's right.
(*ROB touches MAGGY's face. With loving relief, they embrace.*)
An' it's you who's done it, Joe.

JOE: Rubbish.

JED: Ay, don't be ridiculous, Rob. What are you pretendin' for?

MAGGY: He ent pretendin'. Look into his eyes.

SIMON: (*In awe.*) Can you really...see us, Rob?
(*ROB nods.*)

BETH: You sure you're not imaginin' it?

133

ROB: God, I hope not.

JOE: Rob, where am I pointing?

(*Pause.*)

ROB: Right between my eyes.

(*Pause.*)

BETH: You've cured him!

ROB: Yer arm still looks blurred. 'S'if there's a...haze between us. But I can see you.

SIMON: That's one of the most wonderful things I've heard a body say in my whole life.

MAGGY: 'S'a miracle, a copper-bottomed miracle!

BETH: Hallelujah, Halle-lu-jah!

(*JOE backs away from JED.*)

JOE: Now don't *you* start looking at me like that!

JED: You *are* different from the rest of us, aren't you?

JOE: No. This is a case of mass hysteria. A whole week of sunny days is obviously too much for you all. The heat's addled your brains.

JED: But as Beth said earlier, who's responsible for this sweat-box?

JOE: Yes well, as I said...I think I'd better be on my way...

(*JOE moves through the VILLAGERS. They remain motionless but their eyes follow him. He rounds on them.*)

Look, what the hell's happening here?

MAGGY: You. You're what's happening.

JOE: (*Trying to ward her off.*) Maggy...

JED: You do seem to have the power to make life possible for us.

JOE: It's an illusion!

JED: You may not want the power, but it's obviously inside you.

JOE: The lightning could've killed Rob!

ROB: It didn't, though. It cured me.

JOE: Either way, I didn't summon it.

(*They continue to stare at him expectantly.*)

There must be a rational explanation. There has to be.

(*SIMON and BETH exchange smiles, then shake their heads in unison.*)

SIMON: Why does there have to be a rational explanation?

JOE: Because!

(*Pause.*)

JED: I can think of a rational explanation.

JOE: Yes?

(*JED picks up ROB's now-blackened walking stick*)

JED: The bolt of lightnin' earthed itself, usin' this as a conductor.

(*JED snaps the stick.*)

See, it's nuthin' but charcoal.

ROB: Why'd you do that? I've still got a twisted ankle.

JED: (*Discarding the broken stick.*) The electrical current must've surged through Rob with such force that instead of killin' him, by some metabolic quirk, it jolted his paralysed cells back to life again. The cells which control his ocular faculties. It's not that extraordinary. I read of such a case a couple of years back, where a man regained his sight in a storm. Whether he *kept* his sight, of course, is another matter.

JOE: (*Laughing with relief.*) What did I tell you?

BETH: (*Popping another sweet in her mouth.*) That's odd.

MAGGY: What is?

BETH: Scarce a cloud in the sky now.

SIMON: Be a gorgeous sunset.

ROB: Ay; an' haven't I missed 'em. Two whole years without seein' the Heavens on fire. The loss. Can't begin to tell you of the loss.

(*Pause.*)

JOE: Yes...well... (*Offering his hand to ROB who carefully takes it.*) ...goodbye, Rob.

MAGGY: You can't leave us, Joe, we need you!

ROB: (*Refusing to let go of JOE's hand.*) The village won't survive without you. Nor will I.

JOE: (*Pulling his hand free.*) Don't be ridiculous.

JED: (*Half smile.*) You lead. We'll follow.

JOE: (*Laughing.*) Okay, Jed, you've had your fun.

BETH: We'll follow you anywhere.

JED: Even up the mountain. For your sermon.

JOE: (*Still laughing.*) Oh c'mon, Jed, I'm not some sort of...

JED: (*Helpfully.*) ...Modern Messiah?

(*Pause.*)

JOE: You don't believe that!

JED: Might suit me to believe it. Then what?

JOE: You're sick, you're all...

MAGGY: (*Clutching his wrist.*) Why'd you keep denyin' what you've done for us?

JOE: Because I haven't done anything.

ROB: Since you've come here, only good things have happened to Seafall.

JOE: (*Freeing himself from their grasping hands.*) Yes, but like Jed said, it's a coincidence that...

SIMON: (*Interrupting.*) No! There've been too many coincidences for you to just dismiss 'em.

(*Distraught, JOE stretches out his arms to hold the VILLAGERS at bay – even though they are only crowding him with their words.*)

JOE: All right, all right. Maybe they are not coincidences but they still have nothing to do with me.

JED: But if we believe they have everything to do with you, and if we put all our faith in you; perhaps we'll continue to invest you with superhuman powers that would otherwise remain latent inside you. Then what will you do?

(*JOE starts packing his rucksack.*)

JOE: I can't stay here. Or I'll end up as deranged as the rest of you.

BETH: (*Pleading.*) You can wait 'till Monday, surely?

JOE: (*Still packing.*) Why should I?

BETH: If you go now, you'll miss our Spring Festival.

JOE: Spring Festival?

SIMON: Yes, and the kids'll be disappointed if you don't take part in it.

JOE: Oh, the kids are involved, are they?

MAGGY: Ay. Only this mornin' our two asked special if you was goin' to make somethin' for the Festival. (*To ROB.*) Didn't they, luv?

ROB: Asked twice.

JOE: What do they want me to make exactly?

BETH: Last year Simon here made 'em a great wooden bunny rabbit.

JOE: (*Laughing in disbelief.*) What?

SIMON: (*Laughing.*) Ay. Then I climbed on the back of my bunny and rode it.

JOE: Must've been a pretty funny spectacle.

JED: Was a spectacle and a half.

JOE: I'll bet.

MAGGY: So you will make 'em somethin', won't you, Joe?

JOE: (*Shrugging.*) Suppose I could make 'em... I don't know...a wooden horse?

SIMON: Got to have wheels on it.

JOE: Wheels are no problem.

JED: Then you will stay on for our Festival?

JOE: What else happens in this festival of yours?

MAGGY: We sing a lot of chants.

JOE: What kind of chants?

ROB: They're part of the surprise.

JOE: I don't know whether I'm up to anymore surprises.

BETH: The Festival surprises are lovely. Ent they, Simon?

SIMON: Too right they are.

MAGGY: (*Taking JOE's hand.*) Just say you'll stay on, Joe, an' we won't say another word. (*To ROB.*) Will we, luv?

ROB: Not another word, not another word.

JOE: I'll have to think about it.

BETH: If nuthin' else, Joe, stay on for the kids.

JOE: I'll see.

MAGGY: (*Touching his shoulder and looking into his eyes.*) Please. (*Pause.*)

JOE: All right.
(*Everyone laughs and cheers.*)
I'll stay on for your Festival. But as it's only three days away, I'm afraid my Trojan horse won't be very classy.

MAGGY: I'm sure it will. Anyway, it's the thought that counts.

JED: Indeed it is. Well, now that's settled, we'll leave you in peace. At least for the moment.
(*ROB grabs JOE's hand and shakes it vigorously.*)

ROB: Joe, I wish I could find the words to thank you.

(*JOE extricates his hand and massages it to restore the circulation.*)

SIMON: We're goin', we're goin'.

BETH: Ay, we'd best be gettin' back.

(*They start to move off.*)

JOE: (*Waving.*) See you.

MAGGY: (*To ROB.*) Our two are bound to be clamourin' for their tea

ROB: (*To JOE.*) Ay, an' once I tell 'em you're goin' to make 'em a right royal stallion, they'll be as pleased as punch.

(*The VILLAGERS go. JOE turns to the angel and addresses it.*)

JOE: What a loopy village.

(*He uncorks the wine and takes a hefty swig. Chuckling, he picks up the angel and props it against the stern of the boat. Then he offers the angel a drink of wine.*)

Care for a swig?

(*The angel doesn't respond.*)

Suit yourself.

(*JOE takes another swig. Behind him there is the unmistakable rattle of falling pebbles as they slither down the rock-face. JOE whirls round, only to see SANDRA approaching.*)

Sandra! (*Laughing.*) You startled me.

SANDRA: You've done everything for them. But nuthin' for me.

JOE: (*Mystified.*) I'm sorry.

SANDRA: Ma Haxton says you only got to put yer hand on me… (*Indicating her womb.*) …an' I'll be blessed with a baby.

JOE: She's talking nonsense again.

SANDRA: Please!

JOE: I'm sorry, Sandra, but I can't be held responsible for fostering any more of these superstitious fantasies.

(*SANDRA touches his face.*)

SANDRA: You can do anythin' you like to me, Mister.

JOE: (*Backing away from her*) Sandra!

SANDRA: 'S'alright. I've talked it over with me husband. An' he says if it's the only way we can have a child, then…

JOE: You don't know what you're saying.

(*JOE moves away but SANDRA pursues him.*)

SANDRA: If you only knew how long we've prayed for a baby, you wouldn't be so cruel.

JOE: I don't mean to be cruel…but I can't.

(*Tearfully SANDRA runs off. JOE calls after her.*)

Sandra, there's no need to run off like that. Sandra!!

(*Wryly he addresses the angel.*)

Me, an angelic stud. Oh Jesus!

(*Laughing and shaking his head, JOE walks past the boat and disappears along the beach – in the opposite direction to SANDRA.*

Gulls squawk overhead, flying inland, while the angel at the helm of the boat continues to gaze impassively at the hissing sea.)

End of Part One.

PART TWO

Scene 1

Seafall Beach.

Three days later.

Towards sunset.

In the centre of the deserted beach, there is a trestle table with benches either side of it. A white cloth, decorated with garlands of flowers, covers the contents of the table.

On the cliff top, the VILLAGERS can be heard chanting.

VILLAGERS: Hail to the King of the Spring.
  Hail! Hail! May the King bring a burgeoning
  Summer after the Spring.
  Then he'll return in the Fall as the Harvest King!
  Hosanna! Hosanna! Hosanna!
  (*This is followed by the sound of the seagulls squawking above the lapping waves.*
  JED and ROB come into view, each carrying a seven-branched candlestick. They place the candlesticks in the centre of the table.)

ROB: Didn't think he go through with it.

JED: (*Nodding and grinning.*) He still thinks it's a game.
  (*JED lights the candles.*)

ROB: He looked mighty embarrassed sittin' on that wooden horse of his, didn't he?

JED: Ay. (*Pointedly.*) But didn't he remind you of someone?

ROB: So you did hear what my little uns said 'bout him, then?

JED: 'Course. (*Suddenly.*) Duck! Duck!
  (*ROB ducks and bangs his knee against a bench.*)

ROB: Ouch! Why?

JED: (*Laughing.*) That seagull nearly bombed you.

ROB: (*Ruefully rubbing his knee.*) One of the few advantages of bein' blind was I never knew when I was bein' crapped on.

JED: You've got yer sight back one hundred percent, then?

ROB: (*Shaking his head.*) Always a bit blurry when dusk falls. But I believe it's only 'cause he's still here that I can still see.

(*JED is by the sea's edge, sifting sand between his fingers.*)

JED: You goin' to try an' stop him leavin', then?

ROB: Hope it won't come to that.

JED: But if it did?

ROB: (*Rummaging in his pockets.*) Blast.

JED: What's the matter?

ROB: Forgotten me pipe.

(*JED offers ROB a cigarette paper and his tobacco tin.*)

JED: Try one of these.

ROB: (*Peering into the twilight.*) What?

JED: (*Realising.*) You can hardly see at all, can you?

(*ROB feels for the edge of the table and sits on the bench.*)

ROB: It's only come twilight that I have trouble makin' things out.

(*ROB laughs. JED looks at him.*)

Sorry. It's just I can't get over that for three whole days now I've been able to go out fishin' with Simon. Catches we've had have been unbelievable. An' the sights! Dolphins leapin' around us in the early mornin', an' everywhere we cast our nets, shoals of cod an' herrin' come squirtin' in.

(*JED chuckles.*)

What's so funny?

JED: You'd do absolutely anythin' to keep your sight, wouldn't you?

ROB: Sometimes I'm not sure 'bout you, Jed.

JED: (*Amused, rolling a cigarette.*) Really?

ROB: Not sayin' you ent been much friendlier since Joe's come here. But you don't really believe in him, do you?

(*JED wanders along the tide-line.*)

JED: He's certainly a fisher of men.

ROB: Ay, but you don't believe that he's...well...?

JED: (*Cutting him.*) I believe he's been sent to save us. If only from ourselves.

(*JED sees MAGGY and JOE in the distance.*)

(*Taking ROB's arm and leading him away.*) Come on.

ROB: Where you takin' me?

JED: You said you'd do anythin' to stop him leavin'.

ROB: I said I hope it wouldn't come to that.

JED: Perhaps the solution is to give your wife a free rein.

ROB: (*Shaken.*) You don't think he wants to...?

JED: (*Half smile.*) Comin'?

ROB: I'll break his bloody neck!

JED: Let's hope it doesn't come to that.

(*They go.*

A breaker crashes against a rock. Then the sea hisses to itself. JOE and MAGGY appear. JOE is wearing a long white cloak, complete with hood. The cloak is off-set by large magenta-enamelled broach. Despite his tattered jeans, sweat shirt and sandalled feet, JOE retains his natural dignity. MAGGY is in a flowing blue summer-dress with huge pockets.)

JOE: (*Tugging at his cloak.*) Help me off with this, will you, Maggy? Makes me look a right charley.

MAGGY: (*Shaking her head.*) It suits you. 'Specially in this light.

JOE: If I don't look a right charley, I certainly feel one.

MAGGY: Well, you shouldn't. You looked wonderful ridin' your wooden donkey. Like a king come to claim his kingdom.

JOE: It isn't a donkey, it's a horse! Anyway, I looked a real noddy on it. How you conned me into riding it, I'll never know.

MAGGY: Weren't me who persuaded you. Was the children, remember?

JOE: (*Still struggling with the cloak.*) Now the pin on this stupid broach's got stuck.

(*She tries to help him.*)

JOE: Careful, you'll prick yourself.

MAGGY: Just tryin' to get it to hang proper.

JOE: (*Moving away from her.*) I don't want it to hang proper – properly! I just want to take it off.

MAGGY: Oh leave it on. 'Least 'till after the Festival Supper. It's part of the tradition.

JOE: Bound to splotch food down it. I'm a messy eater at the best of times. (*He peers under the white cloth that is covering the food on the table.*) Mmm…looks highly appetising.

MAGGY: (*Playfully smacking his fingers.*) Keep the grub covered or the flies'll be all over everythin'.

JOE: Can't I even have a sausage roll? Not had a bite since last night.

MAGGY: (*Shaking her head.*) The King of the Spring always has to fast for at least twelve hours before his ride into his kingdom.

JOE: The ride's over now and my stomach's growling something chronic.

MAGGY: Rest of us've been fastin', too, y'know. It's traditional for us all to break our fasts at the same time.

JOE: Sod tradition. (*Realising what he's said.*) Sorry. Are the children goin' to eat with us?

MAGGY: No, they've not yet been…
(*She stops herself short.*)

JOE: They've not yet been what?

MAGGY: (*Smiling.*) They're not old enough.

JOE: Oh.

MAGGY: Now don't fret. Mrs Allbright's lookin' after 'em for us.

JOE: Yes, why didn't the Lady of the Manor come and watch me making a total ass of myself?

MAGGY: Mrs Allbright's got no time for our village customs but she's very fond of our kids.

JOE: As it's your Spring Festival, I'm surprised the Vicar isn't here?

MAGGY: He never comes.

JOE: Why not?

MAGGY: He don't like…

JOE: What?

MAGGY: Well, he don't like what he calls the Old Religion bein' mixed up with Christianity.

JOE: I still don't see why you postponed the kiddies' procession 'till this afternoon?

MAGGY: We postponed it 'cause you didn't finish makin' the donkey 'till last night.

JOE: The only reason I was late in finishin' the horse off was because you all kept constantly interrupting.

(*JOE is about to move away when MAGGY seizes his hand.*)

MAGGY: You can't leave us, Joe. You can't!

JOE: Now I've finished the angel, there's nothing left for me to stay for. (*Pause.*) Is there?

MAGGY: Ent there?

(*JOE is now close to her.*)

JOE: Ever worn violets in your hair? Or winter jasmine?

MAGGY: (*Smiling.*) You really are a strange man.

JOE: Am I?

MAGGY: (*Indicating the bench.*) Sit down.

JOE: (*Amused.*) Why?

MAGGY: Sit down.

JOE: All right. (*Sitting.*) So? (*Surprised.*) What d'you think you're doing?

MAGGY: Takin' yer sandals off, ent I?

JOE: Whatever for?

(*MAGGY produces a silver phial from one of her voluminous pockets.*)

What've you got there?

MAGGY: Stop askin' fool questions, an' lean back an' enjoy it.

(*She pours the contents of the phial over his feet.*)

JOE: (*Embarrassed.*) I can't let you do this.

MAGGY: (*Mischievously.*) It's probably the only thing you can let me do; so hush up an' savour it. Now don't get all embarrassed.

(*Luxuriantly she strokes the liquid over his feet.*)

There. Soothin', ent it?

JOE: (*Savouring it.*) What is it?

MAGGY: Oil of myrrh.

JOE: Oil of myrrh's for anointing the dead. (*Realising.*) Of course! How stupid of me. (*Removing her hands from his feet.*) You don't fool me, Maggy.
(*She clutches his hands.*)

MAGGY: Take me away with you!

JOE: What?

MAGGY: If only for a little while.

JOE: (*Laughing.*) And you call me strange.
(*Impulsively he kisses her. She only half responds. He releases her.*)

MAGGY: I didn't ask you to do that.

JOE: Liar. Keep still.

MAGGY: Why?

JOE: Your face is shining.

MAGGY: (*Touching his face.*) Your beard's...silky.

JOE: Don't know about that, but at least it's gone beyond the itchy stage.

MAGGY: Last year when Rob had his beard, it were like kissin' a porcupine. Not that we do much of that these days. He sits for hours lookin' inwards. Makes a bleak lover come bedtime.
(*Pause.*)

JOE: The moon's rising.

MAGGY: 'Tis a lovely sight.

JOE: Like a rock pool.

MAGGY: Looks like the moon to me.

JOE: Yes, but if you look at it closely, you'll see the moon is like veined, translucent pool in all that everlasting darkness.

MAGGY: (*Seizing his hand.*) Take me away from here, Joe.

JOE: Oh Maggy, Maggy.
(*They kiss passionately.*)
Long time since I've felt the need to hold anyone.

MAGGY: Then take me away!

JOE: (*Softly.*) How can I?

MAGGY: For a month. A week. Somethin' to remember.

JOE: You can't just run off with me. What about your kids? And Rob would never take you back. He's not that kind of man.

MAGGY: We could take the kids with us.

JOE: Maggy...

(*She silences him with a prolonged kiss.*)

MAGGY: I worship you. You know that.

JOE: Don't be absurd. You don't know enough about me to even love me, let alone worship me.

MAGGY: It's because I don't understand you that I worship you. Why'd you think I bathed your feet?

JOE: That's enough, Maggy!

MAGGY: Why don't you believe in your own power? We do. We'd be burstin' with pride if we could cure folk like you do.

JOE: I'm not listening.

MAGGY: You've got no choice. Christ in Heaven, even Jed has seen the light now, and he says only you can save us.

JOE: Don't let Jed fool you. He's a man who always needs a cause. Before me, it was Communism; but since the Wall came down, he's been without a job. But my point is, he still needs to worship a god of some form – a god that will subsequently fail him. And because Jed can't control you all in any other way, he has decided to promote me as a panacea for the world's ills. But the greatest irony is, that none of you – including Jed – seem to realise that I also am searching for someone, or something, that I can look up to and follow. If only to prove that there is a point in this everlasting trudging between sand and sky.

(*JOE moves down to the sea's edge.*)

The tide is turning. I can still feel the froth of the last wave oozing between my toes. Take your sandals off, Maggy, and join me. It's very...erotic. (*Smiling.*) Go on, be a devil. If nothing else, it's a way of passing the time.

(*MAGGY removes her sandals and joins him.*)

MAGGY: (*Laughing.*) I don't understand half what you say, y'know. But all it sounds very frustratin'.

JOE: Unfortunately over the years, drifting from place to place, I've developed this doubtful habit of talking to myself. Though I wish I didn't always need to rely on words.

(*MAGGY extends her hand to JOE who obliviously stares out to sea.*)

It would be so restful to be an integral part of all this, wouldn't it?

MAGGY: (*Doubtful.*) Dunno 'bout that.

JOE: Oh it would. The sea is an ever-changing garden. Every breaker is a new season. I would find it very reassuring if I were...say, a barnacled rock...here...at the water's edge. Then on a spring evening like this, I, too, could be part of this garden, lapped round and round by each retreating wave. Like the other creatures of the deep, I would be slowly...ever so slowly...worn away by the salt tide, until my bones were silky soft, and oh so fine and small. Then I'd join the other shells that ceaselessly click together in the boiling foam. Until one midnight some lion-maned breaker from the other side of the world would come and swallow me down. Then vomit me up into...this rock pool. (*Smiling at her puzzled expression.*) Well, can't you imagine what a sublime existence a shell has?

MAGGY: Frankly, no.

JOE: I can. (*Mischievously.*) It must be very peaceful being nothing but a shell. (*Winking at her.*) An aesthetically-shaped, rainbow-coloured shell, of course. If you're a shell, you've no responsibilities, no frustrated desires. (*Crouching by the rock pool.*) You simply lie there at the bottom of the pool, with the occasional spider-crab scuttling across you, or a star-fish embracing you... while the brine slurps around you as the moon tugs the tides. Then late one midsummer afternoon an enterprising child dives her eager fingers into your rock pool, and selects you, or what's left of you, and she treads you onto a damp piece of cotton, along with all the other shells she's gathered during her holiday. She ties you around her neck, and proudly shows you off to her aunt who is sitting hunched up in the shade, praying that her sun-burn will go away. Yes...what a divine bracelet we would all make if suddenly some goddess would circle us around her swan-like neck, to celebrate her eternal summer holiday.

(*JOE laughs and MAGGY joins in. Still laughing they embrace but they break when they realise they have an audience.*

SIMON, SANDRA and BETH emerge from the shadow of the cliff.)

SIMON: (*Grinning, to JOE.*) That your sea-side version of the Sermon on the Mount?

(*JED and ROB appear from the opposite direction.*)

JOE: (*Laughing, to cover his embarrassment.*) I didn't realise you were listening or I wouldn't've made such a fool of myself.

JED: More like a watery version of the parable of the Lilies of the Field.

BETH: You know that everything you say carries on the wind, Master.

MAGGY: There ent no wind.

ROB: May be not. But his words have so many meanings, they go on ringin' in yer head long after you've heard 'em. (*Dangerously to MAGGY.*) Don't they, my sweet.

JED: (*Smiling.*) Just like Jesus' sayings.

JOE: Now don't start all that again, Jed.

BETH: (*To the OTHERS, about the table.*) Well, there's no point in imaginin' what's under the cloth. Get it off an' let's get sat round.

JOE: What an excellent idea.

(*The others laugh while SANDRA and MAGGY remove the cloth to reveal a table groaning with food. JED and ROB place the lighted candles in the centre.*)

Mmm…what a truly magnificent spread.

SANDRA: (*To JED.*) Careful! You're spillin' tallow all over them jellies.

BETH: (*Wrapping JOE's knuckles.*) No grabbin' before grace!

MAGGY: You know where you're sittin', so take yer places, everyone.

JED: What d'you think we're doin'?

(*By now the others have taken their places; up right of the table are MAGGY, JED and SANDRA, while up left are ROB and BETH. SIMON is at the bottom of the table.*)

SIMON: Ouch! That's me corn you've got yer foot on, Beth.

BETH: Then take yer great paw off me knee.

(*The others laugh.*)

MAGGY: (*To JOE who is laughing but still standing.*) Ent you goin' to join us?

(*MAGGY indicates the empty place at the head of the table.*)

JOE: If you don't mind, I'd prefer to sit on one of the benches.

ROB: The head of the table's best place for makin' yerself felt.

JOE: I don't want to make myself felt. I just want to eat!

JED: Don't try an' fool us. We all heard you. Even your words are the trigger to power. Or d'you deny that as well?

JOE: Yes! Because I happen to enjoy the sound of my own voice, it doesn't mean... Well, dreaming aloud is not a crime, is it?

(*They stare at him in silence.*)

Look, why don't you give me one of your delicious pasties, Mrs H, and then I'll be on my way, okay?

JED: (*To the others.*) He can't leave us, can he? 'Least not 'till we've eaten.

(*JOE is reaching for a pasty when SANDRA seizes his hand. Then she falls to her knees in front of him.*)

JOE: Sandra, whatever d'you think you're doing?

SANDRA: You're leavin' us 'cause you think we're not grateful, Master right?

JOE: Grateful?

(*JOE tries to free himself from her grasp but SANDRA kisses his hand fervently.*)

For God's sake, Sandra! (*To the others who are calmly watching the proceedings.*) Well, don't just sit there like statues. Take her home. She's got delayed sunstroke. (*To SANDRA.*) You really mustn't kneel like this. It's so demeaning.

SANDRA: I want to kneel.

JOE: (*Still trying to free himself.*) Let go, will you!?

SANDRA: This is the only way I can thank you for answerin' our prayers.

(*JOE wrenches himself free.*)

JOE: That's better. (*To JED.*) You put her up to this, didn't you?

(*JED smiles.*)

ROB: (*To JOE.*) Why don't you stop playin' with us?

JOE: I'm not playing with you.

BETH: You know why she's kneelin' to you.

JOE: I don't know.

MAGGY: She's with child.

JOE: (*Stunned.*) Sandra...? (*Laughing.*) Impossible.

(*SANDRA hugs JOE.*)

SANDRA: That's what I thought, Master. But you changed all that when you touched me.

JOE: (*Breaking away.*) I didn't touch her! (*Desperately to the others.*) I swear I didn't touch her!

SANDRA: With your words, you touched me.

JOE: This is madness, utter madness! How can you possibly be pregnant when three days ago you told me yourself that you...

SANDRA: (*Cutting him.*) That's the wonder of it.

JOE: But how can you be sure?

SANDRA: That night I had a vision.

JED: (*Amused.*) More than a vision.

SANDRA: I had a vision. And the Angel said that God had blessed my womb.

JOE: Oh not another Immaculate Conception! Look, I know you're all desperate to change your miserable lives but there is a limit. Sorry, Sandra, I don't mean to be hurtful, but you're manufacturing this miracle. Admit it.

JED: (*Smiling.*) So the other miracles were genuine?

JOE: No!

(*JOE slumps onto the bench. The others watch expectantly as SANDRA approaches JOE.*)

(*Warding her off.*) Now stop it! All of you! I refuse to play at being the village's Do-It-Yourself-Messiah!

BETH: Then don't play at it, Master. Just be it.

JOE: And I won't be it, either. And I'm no one's 'Master'!
(*Pause.*)
You won't give up, will you? (*To SANDRA who is still hovering.*) For Heaven's sake, woman, sit down and get on with your meal.
(*Reluctantly SANDRA obeys.*)

ROB: Would you give up in our position?

JOE: Why do you need someone else to follow all the time? You should have the courage to stand on your own flat feet, like I'm trying to do. Oh I know we're wedged together on the planet, but in reality, inside each one of us we're all absolutely alone. And the sooner we accept the fact the better.

MAGGY: We've not felt alone since you came.

SIMON: Never been such neighbourliness around here.

JOE: (*Shaking his head.*) My friends, my friends. If you can't bear to live without having someone, or something to pray to, or believe in; then, for pity's sake, go home and pray to...your land, or your crops, or the moon, or the sea. At least they're worth praying to because they genuinely control your lives. But don't involve me. I don't control anything. Not even myself. Or, better still, if you really have to pray; pray to *yourselves.* Be your own gods. Perhaps, inside each of you, there is a messiah trying to get out, trying to bring salvation to your own souls. If you worship yourselves, you will have no one to blame but yourselves when all these so-called miracles come to an end – as they ultimately have to!
(*JOE leaps to his feet, shaking his fist at the heavens.*)
They bloody well have to!
(*The others clap enthusiastically.*)

BETH: That's great. Weren't that great, folks?

OTHERS: (*Continuing to clap.*) Marvellous! Wonderful!

JOE: What the hell are you clapping for?

SANDRA: Still testin' us, ent you, Master?

JOE: Testing?

SIMON: Ay, you want to see if we're the Rock on which you can build yer Church.

JOE: I don't want to build a sodding church! (*To JED.*) How can you sit there listening to this clap-trap?

JED: Although it's hard to credit, I reckon our Simon has seen through you better than the rest of us.
(*JOE laughs in disbelief.*)
No, I'm being serious, Joseph. What if you are deliberately blasphemin' against yourself.

JOE: Okay, okay. You postulate and I'll eat.
(*JOE sits at the head of the table.*)
Can't remember when I've felt so ravenous.
(*He reaches for a pasty but BETH affectionately raps his knuckles.*)

BETH: Naughty, naughty, Master. Mustn't touch.

JOE: Poisoned 'em, have you? To keep me on my toes.

MAGGY: (*Laughing.*) Lord, no! But we never start our Festival Supper 'till the moon's risen full above the sea.

JOE: What?

JED: In the mean time, perhaps you'll allow me to finish my hypothesis concernin' your divine intentions.

JOE: You saying I can't hit those pasties 'till the moon's risen?

JED: (*Relentless.*) An' my hypothesis is that you are deliberately blasphemin' against yourself, in order to test our faith.

JOE: (*Laughing.*) Communal fasting's made you as nutty as the rest of them. No, really. I thought I could rely on your out-dated Marxist cynicism to view events with a logically-jaundiced eye.

JED: You can't get out of it that easy. You still haven't proved to us that you're not who we say you are.
(*Pause.*)

JOE: And who do you say I am? (*Pause.*) Well?

SIMON: You're our Saviour, aren't you?
(*Pause.*)

SANDRA: Well, you have saved us, Master, ent you?

JOE: (*About to rise.*) Yes well, I think I'd better on my way...
(*ROB puts a restraining hand on JOE's shoulder. Gently but firmly ROB pushes JOE back onto the bench.*)

ROB: You can't leave before you've done the Blessin'.

JOE: You threatening me?

JED: (*Smiling.*) 'Course not.

SIMON: No one's laid a hand on you, have they?

ROB: 'Cept friendly like.

SANDRA: No, we're far too grateful to you.

BETH: 'Course we are, Master!

MAGGY: (*Fiercely.*) Let him go, Beth!

SIMON: (*Warning.*) Maggy.

MAGGY: No, it's hopeless, Simon. He don't want to help us.

JOE: That's not true, Maggy. If there was a way I could genuinely help you, I would. But I can't stomach being some kind of walking idol. Especially when I know that this particular emperor has no clothes.

(*JED stands to confront him*)

JED: If we could prove to you that you have the powers of a Messiah but that God is callously playing games with you; would you then re-consider your position in this community?

JOE: 'God playing games with me.' What are you on about, Jed?

JED: Perhaps this time round, God is deliberately makin' it even harder for His Only Son than He did two thousand years ago.

JOE: That'd take some doing. (*Rising.*) Anyway, you don't believe a word you're saying.

(*Again ROB restrains JOE.*)

ROB: Let Jed finish.

JOE: (*To ROB.*) Can't you see? Jed's deliberately investing me with imaginary powers so that he can go on manipulating the rest of you.

JED: Hear me out.

JOE: Why should I?

JED: Because two thousand years ago, at least accordin' to the Gospels, God revealed His Only Son to mankind. Naturally mankind responded to this revelation by crucifyin' His Only Son.

JOE: Yes, but what's that got to do with me being…?

JED: (*Relentless.*) So then God had to reveal His Only Son again to mankind, by raisin' His Only Son from the dead. But although this helped to increase the number of believers in His Only Son, it did little to change the rapacious nature of mankind.

JOE: Where the devil's this all this getting us?

JED: Stop clawin' at your broach an' listen for a minute! What if, now, two thousand years later, God has decided to have another crack at convertin' mankind to the straight'n narrow? But this time God's more wary, and a helluva lot more crafty. So God determines, in His Infinitely Tortuous Wisdom, to reveal His Only Son's identity to – say, half a dozen distraught souls in an isolated fishin' village on the bleak east coast of nowhere.

JOE: (*Amused.*) Even if there *is* a God – which I very much doubt – why the hell would He want to do that?

JED: To see if there is anyone, anywhere on this planet, who is ready for the Ultimate Revelation of God Himself.

JOE: (*Laughing.*) Oh pull the other one, Jed.

JED: (*Smiling.*) It gets funnier. See, God is now so contemptuous of mankind's over-weening cynicism that He decides to test this insignificant village even unto madness, to see if its inhabitants are worthy of such a revelation. So He lashes 'em with bad harvests, cancer, blindness, infertility – until they're literally screaming for miracles. Then, in a quick sun-burst, God releases His Only Son among these villagers. But surprise, surprise; His Only Son is a pathetic shadow of what the villagers expected His Only Son to be!

JOE: Now wait a minute…

JED: (*Overriding him.*) 'Fact most of the time His Only Son appears to be a weak, vacillating, clown-like figure, full of fear and indecision, who continually denies that He is His Only Son. Hilarious, isn't it? God must be killin' Himself with laughter. It's His Idea of a Divine Practical Joke. So God has gone out of His Way to ensure that these villagers are only too ready to receive His Only Son. (*Smiling.*) But just for the hell of it – and I use the words advisedly – God has withheld the knowledge of His Only Son's Identity – from His Only Son.

JOE: (*Laughing.*) What?

JED: I know it sounds vaguely perverse an' marginally contorted, but God is not God for nothing, is He? That's the very reason His Only Son is positive that He isn't His Only Son. Indeed His Only Son goes further an' insists that he's nothin' but a weak, vacillating, fearful, godless unbeliever, who is just passin' through, an' not even doin' that very well.

JOE: (*Coughing with laughter.*) Stop, man, stop. You'll give me a hernia.

JED: Which brings me back to my original hypothesis. Every time you make a cheap jibe, Joseph; how can you be sure you're not unknowingly blasphemin' against yourself? Well you say you don't know why you're here, or what you're doin' with your life, but you have changed our lives. Right, friends?

OTHERS: Right, right.

JOE: (*Wearily.*) I'm sorry but that's just nonsensical-religious-double-think. I wish to God I was the Second Coming! Then at least when I whistled, Isaiah would come streaking down from the clouds in his chariot of fire to rescue me from you lot!

SIMON: (*Clapping.*) That's more like it, Master. Much more like it!

BETH: Ay, Master, that's really got a holy ring to it.

JOE: (*With his disbelieving head in his hands.*) That was a despairing joke, Mrs H, not a declaration of intent.

MAGGY: Oh c'mon, whatever you say. There's part of you that loves all this attention.

JED: An' there's another part of you that enjoys flirtin' with danger.

JOE: You couldn't be more wrong. To prove it – I'll be on my way.

(*ROB and JED rise to confront him.*)

And no one's going to stop me!

ROB: Really?

MAGGY: (*To ROB.*) Don't you dare touch him!

ROB: He's got to stay, luv. Every time he says he's leavin', darkness fills my eyes an' I can't see!

JOE: You're imagining it, Rob.

JED: (*Quietly.*) Will you stay on here an' try to save the village if I give you physical proof of your power? (*Pause.*)

JOE: (*Smiling.*) There's no way you can. Now step aside, Jed, before someone gets hurt.

SIMON: (*Rising to bar JOE's way.*) Sorry, Master, but we daren't let you go.

SANDRA: (*Seizing JOE's hand.*) Don't leave us, Master. Please!

(*JOE snatches his hand free and turns to face ROB who has materialised behind him. ROB moves forward.*)

JOE: If you as much as touch me, Rob...

(*ROB continues to advance.*)

(*Backing away with clenched fists.*) I'm warning you!

MAGGY: (*To ROB as he continues to block JOE's retreat.*) Robert!

JED: Do us one last service before you go.

JOE: No!

MAGGY: (*Pleading.*) Joe.

(*JOE turns to her.*)

Please.

ROB: We beg you.

JOE: There's no service I can do that'll help you.

SIMON: Tell him, Jed.

SANDRA: Yes, tell him.

JED: If you do it, Joseph, I promise you that you will prove to yourself that you are the Messiah. (*Silencing JOE with an upraised hand.*) And the moment after you have performed the Service; in that moment, I prophecy that the Final Revelation of you – to yourself – will illumine this beach an' the sky, 'till even the moon is eclipsed, and the sea silenced.

(*Pause*)

JOE: (*Softly.*) You really believe I have that kind of power?

JED: I know you have.

(*In the middle distance there is a flicker of lightning, then an ominous thunder-growl.*)

If you don't go through with the Service, the Angel of Destruction will overwhelm us.

JOE: (*Laughing.*) 'Angel of Destruction'?

(*More thunder, but nearer.*)

ROB: Ay, an' the Angel's ridin' on the back of that dragon of a storm.

JOE: Couple of cracks of thunder don't make a storm.

SANDRA: Round here they do.

SIMON: This'll be a right bastard an' all. Feel it in my bones.

(*A jagged flash of lightning is followed by more thunder.*)

MAGGY: The cliff can't take another battery of lightnin' like we had on Lady Day.

JOE: (*Shrugging.*) Well, there's nothing I can do to stop it.

JED: Say the Words, an' the storm'll be snuffed out like a candle in the wind.

JOE: What are you talking about?

(*JED produces a pocket Bible.*)

JED: These words.

JOE: No!

BETH: You've every right to say 'em.

JOE: No. Get your Vicar to say 'em. The Bible's his province, not mine.

SANDRA: We've no use for him no more.

ROB: So you've got to say 'em, Master.

(*The sky is now alive with lightning.*)

JOE: It'd be an act of sacrilege!

JED: How can it be sacrilege, Joseph? You keep tellin' us you don't believe.

JOE: I don't!

(*The lightning is now directly overhead, followed by another crack of thunder.*)

ROB: If you don't even try to help us, an' this storm shatters the cliff, it'll be on your conscience for the rest of yer life.

JOE: (*Trying to control his wind-whipped cloak.*) The storm won't harm the cliff.

SANDRA: Have mercy on us, Master!

JOE: (*Turning away.*) Oh God.

MAGGY: He won't take the cup away – Master.

ROB: No more than He did the last time you were in the
    Garden.

JOE: How many times do I have to tell you? I am not the
    Messiah!

BETH: I'm kneelin' to you, Master.

SANDRA: So am I.

SIMON: An' me.

ROB: An' me – Master.

MAGGY: (*Touching the hem of JOE's cloak.*) An' me.
    (*All the VILLAGERS, save JED, are now on their knees.
    Forked lightning screeches above them while the thunder and
    the wind battle with one another.*)

JED: If it takes kneelin' to convince, I'll kneel. An' I've
    never knelt to man or god before.
    (*JED kneels.*)

JOE: No! Anyone but you.

JED: Then say the words – Master.

JOE: All right, all right! I'll say anything you like as long
    as you get off your knees and stop this!
    (*Pause. Then JED stands. The others follow suit.*)
    That's better.
    (*JED hands JOE the pocket Bible. JOE seems to be a corona
    of fire in the wake of the lightning.*)

JED: Well, say the words, man, before the heavens fry us
    alive!
    (*JED points to a certain passage.*)

JOE: (*Appalled.*) Not this!

ROB: You promised, Master.

JOE: You can't expect me say this!

SANDRA: You swore you would, Lord!
    (*The storm sets the bells jangling in the church on the cliff.*)

JED: SAY IT! Or we'll have the bloody cliff down on top of
    us!
    (*JOE backs away.*)
    Say the words.

MAGGY: Yes, say 'em.

EVERYONE: For God's sake, say the words and save us!
    SAVE US!

JOE: (*Trying to make himself heard above the thunder.*) 'With desire... I have desired to eat the passover with you... before I suffer. For I say unto you...

(*JOE breaks off as a screeching bolt of lighting electrifies the cliff. There is the sound of falling rocks to their left.*)

MAGGY: Please, Joseph!

JED: What's it cost if you don't believe.

SIMON: Just say the words an' we'll do the believin' for you.

OTHERS: (*In a crescendo of desperation.*) Please, Master, PLEASE!

(*There is now total war in Heaven.*)

JOE: (*Shaking his fist at the lightning.*) All right, you win, God damn you! (*Reading at the top of his voice in order to be heard over the elemental tumult.*) 'With desire I have desired to eat this passover with you before I suffer. For I say unto you, I will not eat any more thereof, until it be fulfilled in the Kingdom of God.' (*To the others.*) I don't see what good this is doing!

JED: If you'd listen to yourself instead of shoutin' at us, you'd hear Your Father pullin' the storm back from Seafall.

(*BETH, who has poured some wine into JOE's glass, passes the glass to JOE. Almost in a trance, JOE holds up the glass in the candlelight.*)

JOE: 'Take this and divide it among yourselves.' (*His voice is noticeably unsteady.*) 'For I say unto you, I will not drink of the fruit of the vine, until the Kingdom of God shall come.'

(*BETH takes the glass from JOE. SANDRA hands him a piece of bread. With trembling hands, JOE breaks the bread.*)

(*Whispering.*) 'This...is my body which is given to you; this do...in rememberance of me.'

(*JOE places a crumb of bread on BETH's tongue. Then he passes crumbs of bread to the OTHERS who are kneeling.*)

(*Half laughing/crying.*) Forgive us for we know not what we do.

JED: There are more words. Say them.

(*BETH passes JOE his glass of wine.*)

JOE: (*No longer reading, but from memory.*) 'This cup is the new testament – in my blood, which is sent for you.'
(*JED reaches out for the glass but JOE refuses to give it him.*)

JED: But...?

JOE: (*Cutting him, and still from memory.*) 'But behold, the hand of him that betrayeth me, is with me on the table. And truly the Son of Man goeth, as it was determined, but woe unto that man by whom he is betrayed.'
(*Pause.*)

JED: (*Shaken.*) I never will betray you!
(*JOE turns away from JED and gives the wine to BETH. She drinks, and is about to pass it to MAGGY when MAGGY realises that JOE has slumped back in his chair. Concerned, MAGGY kneels beside JOE and touches his face.*)

MAGGY: You're...cryin', ent you?

JOE: The words are so beautiful. Filled with such love... and power. For a moment they moved me, that's all.
(*Trying to laugh.*) Last time I heard them was...
(*He trails off.*)

JED: When?

JOE: Doesn't matter. I still had no right to say them.

ROB: You had every right.

SIMON: Ay, 'twas only your words that saved the village from bein' destroyed by the storm just now.

BETH: Don't weep, Master.

MAGGY: No, you mustn't cry.

JOE: Didn't mean to. It's just...for a moment then...while I was actually saying the words, I...well, I suddenly felt...
(*Distraught JOE breaks off and stares out to sea.*)

SANDRA: What, Master?

JOE: I suddenly felt...well, I wondered if...

JED: You need not wonder. You are the Chosen One. We have chosen you.
(*JOE lurches to his feet, accidentally knocking his glass onto the shingle. SIMON is about to retrieve it.*)

JOE: Leave it! (*Backing away.*) I refuse to be your Chosen One, d'you hear me?

SIMON: Who else but God's Only Son could've snuffed out that storm?

JOE: The storm snuffed itself out! My little 'moment' was yet another delusion. I'm just like the rest of you. Always seeking, but without ever knowing what I'm seeking. Why won't you accept it? (*To JED.*) You can't say I didn't warn you.

JED: Warn me?

JOE: About your 'revelation', that was supposed to 'illumine the beach and sky'. It hasn't 'revealed' itself, has it? The moon isn't eclipsed, and the sea hasn't stopped hissing.

JED: But there was a sudden moment, wasn't there? – when you broke your body, and blessed your blood.
(*JOE turns away.*)
And in that moment, you said you felt something.
(*Again JOE stares out to sea.*)

ROB: Tell us what you felt.

BETH: Share it with us, Master.

MAGGY: Yes, tell us, Master.

TOGETHER: Please, Master! Please!

JOE: (*After a pause.*) I know it doesn't make sense, but in that moment I had a dazzled glimpse of...the enormity of what it is...to even think of being God. The very idea hurls the mind into an abyss. But as I broke the bread and blessed the wine, it was as if I was being...devoured by the raw power of God. But no words can come anywhere near to expressing such a revelation. All I know is, that for one wondrously fearful moment, I experienced a little, a very little of what He must have experienced during His Last Supper. It was not simply an apprehension of Divine Terror – although there was terror – nor the electrifying possibility that I could, by an act of belief, stream supernatural lightning from my finger ends...no, it was something more than all these. I was possessed – as He must have been possessed – with the desire to embrace each and everyone of you, your village, and every man, woman and child along this coast, and inland, in the mountains, the towns...yes, embrace you all! Like a fire embraces a forest. Consuming your dry leaves and your sapless bark until your very souls are as incandescent as your eyes are in the darkness now. In that moment I knew that once the flames of love had consumed you, each of your souls would shine forth in its own right. Then never again would you mindlessly crave the Revelation of God's Divine Fire. Never again would you flirt with miracles and omens. At last you would be free to take responsibility for your own lives. Instead of always wanting to be lead by someone like me! Who is even more blighted than you are. So, for God's sake, let me go now while there's still time for all of us.

(*Pause.*)

Please. PLEASE!

(*Long pause.*)

ROB: Don't leave me, Master, or the darkness'll take me.

JOE: (*To ROB.*) I have no choice. (*Turning to SIMON.*) You once said I could borrow your old rowing boat any time I needed it.

SIMON: Ay, Master, but…

JOE: I need it now.

JED: What for?

JOE: I'm going to row along the coast to East Haven.

SIMON: Oh no you're not.

JOE: You can collect the boat from there in a couple of days.

SIMON: You can't…!

JOE: (*Cutting him.*) If you want your bumper catches to continue, you will oblige me.

(*The others press silently towards him.*)

Don't any of you try to stop me. Especially you, Jed. Or I shall call the storm back. And you won't like that.

MAGGY: You can't simply…

JOE: (*Interrupting.*) Watch me.

ROB: You'll never make it along the coast. The currents are treacherous as hell.

BETH: And if they don't get you, the Sunken Village will rip the bottom of your boat to shreds.

JOE: I bear a charmed life. (*Smiling.*) Or didn't you know? Well, goodbye, my friends. And God, if by some eternal fluke, You should happen to exist, try to have mercy on us all.

(*JOE moves to go. MAGGY throws her arms around his neck.*)

MAGGY: Please, take me with you!

(*JOE extricates himself.*)

JOE: No.

(*JOE goes. There is a long pause of indecision.*)

SANDRA: We must bring him back.

JED: No need.

MAGGY: If we don't bring him back, then…?

JED: He's already exhausted.

ROB: What difference does that make?

JED: He won't be able to row far tonight.

SIMON: (*Nodding.*) Don't reckon he'll make the Sunken Village.

JED: An' one stroke after midnight; it's tomorrow.

BETH: What's special about tomorrow?

JED: (*Grinning.*) You'll see. (*Sitting down at the table.*) Well, there's no point leaving all this excellent food for the Lord of the Flies. (*To BETH.*) If you play mother, Mrs H, we'll all get stuck in.

(*JED starts to eat with gusto. Laughing, the others join in. Only MAGGY remains on the tide-line, gazing after the retreating JOE…as the light fades.*)

Scene 2

A sheltered cove overlooking the remains of the Sunken Village.

Before dawn. The following morning.

It is still dark but the rocks and sea seem unnaturally luminous under the setting moon.

There is a rowing boat, covered with tarpaulin, on the shingle.

A seabird gives a disconsolate call, heading inland.

Silence, other than the sound of the sea. This is broken by a handful of pebbles skittering down the cliff-face.

Pause. Two FIGURES, hooded in sou'westers, appear on opposite sides of the cove. Stealthily they converge on the rowing boat. The slighter of the two is armed with a shotgun. His burly companion carries a glowing lantern.

The FIGURE WITH LANTERN wrenches the tarpaulin off the boat. There is a cry from beneath. Then JOE's startled face jerks into view.

JOE: What the devil's going on?

FIGURE WITH GUN: Sorry. Thought you were a fox.

JOE: Do I look like a fox?

FIGURE WITH LANTERN: Perhaps you'd be good enough to step out of the boat, so's we can check the colour of yer tail.

JOE: (*Laughing and yawning.*) I've had bizarre requests in my time but this takes the gingerbread.
(*JOE climbs out of the boat. A small book falls from his lap onto the shingle.*)
So what can I do for you, gentlemen?
(*The FIGURE WITH GUN retrieves the book.*)

FIGURE WITH GUN: Bible-reader?

JOE: I was glancing through it when I dropped off. And that's what you intended I should do – right, Jed?
(*Pause.*
Indicating the FIGURE WITH LANTERN.) And it was Samson here who hid the Bible in my rucksack.
(*The FIGURES throw back their hoods – to reveal the grinning faces of JED and ROB respectively.*)

JED: Glad you still remember us.

ROB: (*Rubbing his eyes.*) Incredible, just incredible.

JOE: (*Yawning.*) What's 'incredible'?

ROB: Last couple of days I've scarce been able to see a thing. An' the moment you left us, Master, I went godnear blind. But now I can see the manes of them sea-horses rompin' over the Sunken Village, like it were noontide.

(*ROB grabs JOE's wrist.*)

I won't go through that hell again, y'hear me?

JOE: (*Struggling.*) You're bruising my arm.

ROB: You got to come back with us, Master.

JOE: Let go of me!

(*JOE wrenches his arm free and stumbles back against the boat.*)

I'm so tired. Could sleep standing up.

(*JED rolls a cigarette.*)

JED: Could've sworn the fox came this way.

JOE: What fox?

JED: 'Fact there were a couple of 'em.

ROB: (*Lighting his pipe.*) Killed half my chickens, they did.

JOE: (*Sarcastic.*) Perhaps they went for a midnight swim around the Sunken Village. Oh didn't you know? All scavengers have an Atlantis complex.

(*JED flicks through the Bible.*)

JED: You stole this durin' your Last Supper, didn't you?

JOE: I didn't steal anything!

JED: (*Pointing sea-ward.*) To think the Sunken Village used to be a thrivin' community. That was the village shop. Blacksmiths. 'Sailor's Arms'.

JOE: D'you mind reminiscing somewhere else?

(*JOE subsides on a rock and appears to go to sleep.*)

JED: An' to the left of that rock was my folk's cottage.

ROB: Where them cormorants are swimmin'?

JED: Ay. Now all that's left are a few chunks of stone wreathed in miles an' miles of seaweed. (*To JOE.*) No point in pretendin' you're asleep, Joseph. We know you've been waiting for us.

JOE: Last thing I've been doing is waiting for you two. Anyway, how did you know where to find me?

JED: Not even us locals are daft enough to try an' negotiate the Sunken Village after dusk. An' we're not alone in findin' you.

JOE: What d'you mean?

(*JED points to a large piece of driftwood.*)

JED: This cross-beam was ripped off the church in the storm. (*Indicating ROB.*) Like us, it's been searchin' for you, too.

JOE: (*Laughing.*) That lump of wood's been 'searching' for me?

ROB: Ay, Jed, what are you gabbin' about?

JED: If this cross-beam wasn't searching for you, why did it choose to get itself washed up here?

JOE: You're really turning into a very boring clown, Jed.

JED: Am I?

JOE: Yes, because you're not making any sense. Even by your own dubious standards.

JED: (*Touching the beam with his foot.*) Prop it up against the boat, Rob.

ROB: Why?

JED: Prop it up an' you'll see.

ROB: All right.

(*ROB picks up the cross beam and carries it to the boat.*)

JED: You believe in signs, don't you?

JOE: Signs?

(*ROB props the cross beam up against the boat.*)

God in Heaven, it's just like…

ROB: …Our Lord's Cross.

JED: It's a little crooked, of course. But then God has never been overly fond of the straight an' narrow. At least not as far as His nearest and dearest are concerned.

JOE: (*Laughing.*) So it looks a bit like a cross; so what?

JED: It's a miraculous sign – that has been sent to stir your memory.

ROB: You're right, Jed. (*To JOE.*) An' you know what this cross demands, Master.

JOE: Don't call me that.

ROB: Ever since you broke your body and blessed your blood, you've been prayin' we'll find you…

JED: …An' dreadin' our comin'.

JOE: (*Moving away from them.*) That's a crazy lie and you know it.

ROB: Turnin' yer back on us won't change nuthin'.

JED: Yes, 'cause this cross is waitin' to fulfil its divine function.

(*JED prods JOE with his gun.*)

JOE: D'you mind pointing that in another direction? It's making me fractionally jumpy.

JED: Sit down.

JOE: I don't want to sit down.

ROB: (*Looming over him.*) He said sit down!
(*JOE sits.*)

JED: You might as well admit it.

JOE: Admit what?

JED: You know only too well what you've done for Rob an' the rest of the village. An' while you were out there fighting the sea, you came to terms with the consequences.

JOE: All these so-called miracles that you say I performed were fortuitous accidents. Coincidences!

ROB: (*To JED.*) Seems he still needs the final proof.

JOE: Proof?

JED: That you are who we say you are.

JOE: Listen, I'm really too tired for all this.

ROB: An' there's no better day than today to prove it.

JOE: What's today?

JED: (*To ROB.*) He knows what today is.

JOE: I don't know.

ROB: That's why you've waited for us.

JOE: (*Laughing.*) You're both insane.

JED: On the contrary, we are the ones left who are sane.

ROB: Only ones with any guts.

JOE: What, in God's name, do you want of me?

ROB: 'S'your day. You choose.

JOE: My day?

JED: Good Friday.

JOE: It can't be.

JED: You know it is.

ROB: You can't've forgotten the last time you were stretched out against the dawn.

JED: (*Putting his arm around JOE's shoulder.*) Starin' out to sea won't help you, Master. Every wave breakin' will only bring back the taste of vinegar on your lips. An' the seaweed is the thorns gaugin' inwards towards your brain. See that splinter of rock out there. That made the spear wound festerin' in your side. Now the whole weight of your dyin' love is held, between sea an' sky, by three rusty nails – to this.

(*JED strokes the cross-piece.*)

JOE: (*Trying to laugh off his growing fear.*) Well…if you've got some nails, all you need now's a hammer, right?

ROB: It'd clear things up one way or another, wouldn't it?

JOE: Clear what up?

ROB: Whether you are God's Son or not?

JOE: (*Still trying to laugh.*) Talk about Tom O'Bedlam and Crazy Jane.

JED: (*Smiling.*) I believe you are.

JOE: Liar!

ROB: I know you are. My eyes are the livin' proof.

JOE: Don't give me that. It's just psychosomatic.

JED: Take a look in the boat, Rob. Knowin' Simon, he's bound to have some nails somewhere.

ROB: And where there are nails, there's generally a hammer.

JOE: Oh come on, even if you two were insane enough to try and crucify me, how would my death help you or your moon-struck village? Well, it won't help, will it?

ROB: It won't help us. It'll save us. (*Finding a hammer and some nails.*) Bingo!

(*ROB places the hammer and nails in front of JOE. JED sorts through the nails.*)

JOE: (*Laughing uneasily.*) Only on the east coast of nowhere can lunacy be a way of life.

JED: If the Messiah is unaware of His Own Divinity before His Death, He won't be able to deny if after His Resurrection. Then He'll re-appear in the midst of the village, an' save us from His Father's Wrath. As a result, we'll become known as the Village of the Resurrection. And there's nothin' tourists'll like more; so our livelihoods will be ensured.

JOE: You'll both be arrested as homicidal maniacs. Presupposing, of course, that you have the guts to nail me onto this cross in the first place – which you know you haven't.

ROB: Haven't we?

JOE: (*Smiling.*) Have you ever killed a man, Rob?

ROB: No.

JOE: (*To JED.*) Have you?

JED: (*Grinning.*) Only with ideas.

JOE: Exactly. That's why this is nothing but demented nonsense. You don't believe I'll resurrect myself. And even if you did, you're both too cowardly to commit murder for something as ephemeral as belief. Oh I know you're jealous of me, Rob, but there's no need to be because Maggy's just deluding herself.

ROB: Not doin' this out of jealousy. I'm goin' to do it to keep my sight.

JOE: (*Trying to hide his growing desperation.*) Have you thought about the actual process of crucifying me?
(*JOE snatches a nail from JED, then he grabs the hammer and lams a nail into the cross.*)
Imagine physically hammering these nails into the palms of my hands, and driving a wedge of rusty iron into my feet. Then when you've nailed me up, you heave my sobbing weight, on this cross beam, into some cleft in the rock. Then you leave me, screaming my utter disbelief to the incoming tide. Yes, you might well avert your eyes, Rob. Better to be blind again than to gaze on such butchery. Not that you've the stomach for it anyway.

JED: (*Looking him in the eyes.*) You've read the Book of Job, so you know there is no limit to what men will do when their lives are on the edge.

JOE: What's the Book of Job got to do with you crucifying me?

JED: 'My bones are pierced in the night season. I am brother to dragons, and a companion to owls. I meet with darkness in the day time, and grope in the noonday as in the night.' An' that is how we are in Seafall, Joe, now that you've taken your revelations away from us. Whether you like it or not, you electrified us with hope. An' we can't live now without that hope.

JOE: You don't believe that any more than I do!
(*JED picks up the Bible.*)

JED: Wrong. Embedded in here – is our salvation.

JOE: (*Laughing.*) In there?

ROB: Ay. 'Cause the Good Book tells us to be done with dragons an' owls, an' the darkness an' all its creatures. For like it or not, Master; you are the Light! An' if we have to make you suffer so's you can burn more brightly, then make you suffer we will.

JOE: I've suffered more than enough of your craziness!
(*JOE picks up his haversack and starts to leave. ROB throws the Bible at him.*)

ROB: The Truth is in there, an' there's no runnin' away from it.

JOE: (*Shaken.*) God give me inspiration to deal with these madmen.

JED: You're the one who's insane, Master, because you're denyin' yourself. But deep inside, you know who you are.

JOE: (*Frenziedly flicking through the Bible.*) How can I convince you? I can't find it! Yes…now I remember.
(*Without realising what he is doing, JOE quotes from memory.*)
'Take heed that no man deceive you; for many shall come in my name, saying: "I am the Christ." But go not after them. For there shall arise false Christs and false prophets, who shall show you great signs and wonders, but follow them not. For as the lightning cometh out of the east and shineth even unto the west, so shall the Coming of the Son of Man be. Then the sun shall be darkened, the stars shall fall from Heaven, and then – shall appear the sign of the Son of Man.'
(*JOE trails off. In the distance, there is a flicker of lightning.*)

JED: 'And this generation shall not pass away 'till all these things are fulfilled.'

JOE: (*In his own world.*) 'But of that day and hour knoweth no man, no, not the angels in Heaven, but my Father only.'
(*Distraught JOE stares out to sea.*)
What's happening to me?

ROB: You've seen yerself in the turn of the wave.

JOE: What is happening?
(*JED takes a crumpled photograph out of his pocket and gives it to JOE.*)
Where the hell did you get this?

JED: (*Pointing at the photograph.*) That's you. And the fourth from your left is the Vicar, right?

JOE: You've been in my room.

ROB: You weren't coming back, were you?

JED: Once we found it, we rang the Vicar, of course.

ROB: He told us everything.

JOE: All right, I'm not denying that I dropped out of ecclesiastical college because I ceased to believe. But what does that prove?

JED: It proves that God is as perverse as I said He was. And when you've thought it through, you'll realise that now you can never leave us.

ROB: (*Crouching beside JOE.*) I'm sorry I threw the Bible at you, Master. But with you gone, there's nuthin'! You're all we have.

JED: Even if you are an illusion.

(*ROB is now kneeling to JOE who is still staring hopelessly out to sea.*)

ROB: I know you hate us needin' you, but without you, we are lost.

JED: At sunset, we'll take your body off the cross an' place it in a cave.

ROB: Then, come Sunday, you'll rise from the dead an' save us.

(*Appalled, JOE is about to reply.*)

JED: Before you refuse – Master, pray for guidance.

JOE: What?

ROB: Like you did in the Garden of Gethsemane.

JOE: You don't really believe…

ROB: (*Interrupting.*) We believe in you, Master.

JOE: I'm not master of myself, let alone…

ROB: (*Cutting him.*) Wrong. The only reason I can see is because you healed me.

JOE: No.

JED: Beth no longer has cancer because you cured her.

JOE: No!

ROB: Sandra's with child 'cause you touched her.

JOE: No!

ROB: Hidin' yer face won't change nothin'.

JED: The circumstantial evidence makes your lack of faith in yourself absurd.

ROB: Remember your ride on the donkey...

JED: Remember the children shouting Hosannas...

JOE: I only did it to humour all of you!

JED: But remember...

ROB: ...How you broke the bread...

JED: ...And blessed the wine...

ROB: ...And the storm dissolved...

JED: ...Remember how you felt...

ROB: ...Remember your power...

JED: ...Remember...

JOE: HOW CAN I EVER FORGET?

ROB: It's too late to get away from us now, Master.

JED: He doesn't want to get away from us. In his heart he knows that if he deserts us, wherever he goes he'll always hear us cryin' out to him. Even in the wilderness. Every patch of wet sand will have our faces imprinted on it, waitin' for his feet to stamp on our tears. (*To JOE.*) If you don't believe me, pray for the truth. An' all will be revealed.

JOE: How can I pray when I don't know who to pray to?

JED: Follow your own advice. Pray to yourself. (*Tapping his gun.*) We'll be waitin'. An' unlike your last disciples in the Garden, we shan't fall asleep.

(*JED goes. ROB follows.*)

JOE: (*Alone.*) I can't die for a god I don't believe in.
(*In the middle distance there is a flicker of lightning.*)
(*Shouting at the lightning.*) I DON'T BELIEVE IN YOU!
(*Staring out to sea.*) Yet ever since I ceased to believe in you, I have this terrible need to believe in something. I'm not enough, alone. Although being alone may be the ultimate truth. Why can't I accept that my heart-beat is my only life-long companion? Perhaps because the sound of my heart beating in my ears is the one thing that reminds me that I am going to die. All I can do is peer into the depths of my loneliness, which is the same loneliness that haunts everyone in the wolf hours of the night. But knowing we're all rotting away with loneliness

brings no comfort. And knowing we shouldn't need God, that doesn't comfort me either.

(*Pause.*)

If only I was certain that these…'miracles' were merely…accidental Acts of God. Or did I – as they believe – make them happen? Oh help thou my unbelief!

(*Pause.*)

Either blind me with Divine Truth, or leave me in peace to drift away in ignorance. The not-knowing is destroying me!

(*Pause.*)

Well, am I who they say I am? (*Smiling.*) I think not. But as I don't know and they seem so sure, perhaps I should endeavour to find the strength to endure the cross. I know there will be no Resurrection. And when they know it, too, they will be free of me, and forget me. But will my vanity stretch so far to embrace such agony, simply to destroy their faith in me? No! I couldn't bear the pain of nails being driven into my flesh for a single second, let alone… (*Laughing through his tears.*) It's only in legends that men are brave enough to die for *other* people's beliefs. But wouldn't it be wonderful to create a legend? It would be immortality of a kind. And in the process…of dying, who knows, I may create one. Then I would need my disciples. Well, there's only one certain way to find out.

(*JOE moves to the cross that is wedged in the shingle by the boat.*)

(*In a challenging voice.*) 'And there was darkness over all the earth.'

(*JOE looks upwards. The clouds have already obscured the moon. Close by there is a flash of lightning.*)

(*Summoning his 'disciples'.*) 'And behold – the veil of the temple was rent in twain from the top to the bottom.'

(*A crack of thunder. The shadowy figures of JED and ROB materialise in the stormy darkness.*)

'And the earth did quake, and the rocks were rent. And the graves…were opened'!

(*A searing flash of lightning illuminates JOE who is now facing the cross. His arms are stretched out parallel to the silhouette of the cross-beams. For a moment JOE seems to glow in the lightning-glare.*)

There is a deafening crack of thunder.

Blackout.

Scene 3

The same sheltered cove overlooking the Sunken Village.

Pre-dawn darkness. Two days later.

Mist drifts over the beach. The rowing boat has gone. All that remains is the crumpled tarpaulin that covered it.

The cove is silent save for the lapping of the untroubled sea. The silence is broken by the sound of pebbles and small rocks skittering down the cliff-face.

A beat. Then more pebbles, backed by the urgency of approaching voices.

VICAR: (*Off.*) Sure they said down here, Maggy?

MAGGY: (*Off.*) Sunken Village is the Sunken Village, Vicar.

SIMON: (*Off.*) Ay, but it ent yet six in the mornin', gal.
(*Blades of flickering light scissor across the cove. MAGGY and SANDRA emerge out of the mist, brandishing electric torches.*)

SANDRA: Even if they were here, we'd never see 'em in this mist.

MAGGY: Won't be long 'till dawn. Then the mist'll clear.

SIMON: (*Appearing with a torch.*) Still no sign of 'em, then?

SANDRA: 'Fraid not.
(*BETH appears breathless and coughing, with the VICAR giving her support.*)

BETH: They could've at least've held this meetin' after Communion.

VICAR: The whole thing seems unnecessarily bizarre.

MAGGY: (*Calling out.*) Rob? Rob!!

SIMON: (*Calling into the mist in the opposite direction.*) Ay, c'mon, Jed Thomas, this ent no time for hide'n-seek. So stop playin' funny buggers. Beg pardon, Vicar.

SANDRA: Did they really say they wanted us to meet here?

MAGGY: (*Shaking her head.*) They just said we was to come to the Sunken Village before dawn.

BETH: Got to sit down or me old pins'll fold under me.

SIMON: Can't squat there, gal. You'll get pneumonia.

(*BETH is seized by a prolonged coughing fit. The others stare at her.*)

BETH: (*To the VICAR.*) 'S'this drattin' mist.

VICAR: (*Gently.*) Is it?

BETH: (*Still coughing.*) The Master cured me. I tell you, he cured me!

VICAR: Never mind, Mrs Haxton…

MAGGY: Beth's right; the Master has cured her! He has a power beyond all understandin'. Felt it meself; the moment he touched me, floodin' through his arms, his mouth… (*Breaking off in embarrassment.*) I mean…

(*ROB materialises out of the mist, with a lantern.*)

ROB: One thing's certain, wife. You'll never taste his mouth again. No woman will.

MAGGY: Where is he, then?

SANDRA: Ay, where is he?

ROB: (*To SANDRA.*) Why ent Andrew come with you?

SANDRA: We had a row.

ROB: So?

VICAR: Rob!

SANDRA: I don't mind him knowin', Vicar. (*To ROB.*) Andrew thinks I'm not really pregnant. He says I'm in love with the Master, an' he says that's why I said I had this vision. But it's not true.

VICAR: Isn't it?

SANDRA: Well…perhaps I imagined I had this vision, but I am still pregnant. (*Defiant.*) Well, I am!

(*The VICAR shakes his head.*)

SIMON: (*To ROB.*) You know where the Master is, don't
    you?

ROB: (*Nodding and pointing sea-ward.*) Out there.

VICAR: Look, what the devil's all this about?

(*JED enters pale and unshaven.*)

JED: You'll find out soon enough.

ROB: Where have you been, Jed?

(*In his agitation, ROB stumbles over the crumpled tarpaulin.
Helping ROB to his feet, the VICAR accidentally pulls the
tarpaulin back to reveal – a wooden cross.*)

VICAR: Good God!

JED: Let's hope He is, Vicar.

SIMON: (*Indicating the cross.*) What's this doin' here?

JED: (*To ROB who is now fiercely rubbing his eyes.*) Well, tell
    'em, man. It's what they've come for.

ROB: I can't see proper. 'S'all blurred.

SANDRA: Don't give into doubt, Rob.

BETH: Yes, you must go on believin', Rob! Then yer
    sight'll come back. (*Breaking down.*) It has to come back,
    it has to!

(*BETH crumples to her knees. The VICAR and SIMON go
to her.*)

VICAR: Don't cry, Mrs Haxton.

SIMON: Ay, chin up, lass.

JED: You're right, Ma; Belief is everythin'. An' it's because
    Rob an' I believe, that we did what we did.

MAGGY: What are you saying?

BETH: (*To JED, in disbelieving whisper.*) You haven't!
    (*Kneeling by the cross.*) No… I don't believe you.

VICAR: Of course they haven't. This is the twenty-first
    century. People don't do things like that.

(*Before JED can respond, SIMON rushes down to the sea's
edge, gesticulating.*)

SIMON: That's my boat out there!

MAGGY: (*Joining him.*) Where?

SIMON: Comin' out of that patch of mist.

SANDRA: Who's in it?

SIMON: I can't see. What's the damn fool doin'? Tide'll rip
    it onto the rocks.

JED: No! Nothing will hurt the boat.

BETH: (*To JED.*) I know who's in it.

JED: There's nobody in it. Nobody alive.

SANDRA: (*Turning on JED.*) You really have killed him, ent
you? (*Shaking JED.*) Ent you?!

VICAR: Of course they haven't.

ROB: With these hands. In the Wolf Hour on Good Friday.

VICAR: I don't believe you.

SANDRA: Nor do I.

SIMON: (*Overlapping.*) Why did you do it, Rob?
(*ROB looks at MAGGY.*)

MAGGY: (*Shaking her head.*) No, not for that!

BETH: It can't be true.

SIMON: Why did you do it?!

JED: Because the rest of you hadn't the guts! Like always
you want to live contented lives, but you don't care that
other poor souls have to suffer so's you can. Don't look
indignant. You all wanted the Master to stay on an' save
Seafall, but because you're so soft-gutted an'
'neighbourly', you left the blood-lettin' to me and Rob.
You still don't believe me, do you? That boat out there
will survive the rocks, Simon. Then you'll see the
Master's mangled corpse for yourself. Right, Rob?

VICAR: You've taken this obscene fantasy far enough.

JED: We were at our wits' end, weren't we, Rob?

ROB: Yes. We wanted to believe that if we crucified him, he
would rise from the dead an' save our village, but...

JED: (*Interrupting.*) So the moment the sun touches the
Master's body, he will cast off his death, an' walk on the
water to embrace you all – just as he prophesied he
would at his Last Supper.
(*The VICAR shivers.*)

SANDRA: Someone step over yer grave, Vicar?

VICAR: (*Shading his eyes and looking sea-ward.*) Trick of the
light. Has to be.

BETH: No! Some'at is movin' in the boat...

VICAR: (*Relieved laughter.*) It's just a flock of gulls.

MAGGY: Sun's made their wings all golden.

BETH: Ay, but there's…someone standin' in the middle of
'em.

SIMON: Where?

BETH: (*Pointing.*) In the prow of the boat.
(*Pause.*)

SIMON: I think you're right, Beth.

ROB: (*Shaking his head.*) Impossible.

JED: (*Hard.*) Rob!
(*ROB shakes his head again.*)

BETH: The Master is in the boat, Rob. Or can't you see
nothin' no more?

ROB: I don't have to see. I know the truth.

JED: Rob!

VICAR: (*Shading his eyes.*) The glare's too dazzling to see
anything properly.

BETH: The Master's comin' back to us, I tell you!

ROB: Beth, I want to believe in his resurrection as much as
the rest of you, but the boat is empty!

BETH: How can you say that? His cloak is flappin' like a
great white flag out there. He's risen from the dead – for
us!

MAGGY: No…the only thing that's risen is the sun.

VICAR: Absolutely.

SANDRA: There's definitely no one out there.

ROB: 'Course he isn't there! He couldn't possibly have risen
from the dead.

JED: Be quiet!

ROB: Well, how could he? When we didn't have the guts to
crucify him in the first place.

JED: Damn you!

ROB: (*Pointing to JED.*) It were his idea. Weren't it?

SIMON: What was?

ROB: They've a right to know the truth, Jed.

MAGGY: (*Realising.*) You mean…this is all a sick joke?

ROB: We didn't mean it to be. No use strainin' yer eyes,
Beth. There's nothin' out there but the sun risin'.

SIMON: Did the Master…run away, then?

ROB: No. We did. (*To JED.*) Didn't we, teacher?

BETH: Is that true, Jed Thomas?

(*JED turns to face his ACCUSERS.*)

JED: I only did it to give us all some hope. Somethin' to go
　　on believin' in.

SIMON: You ran away?

(*JED nods.*)

ROB: When we'd got far enough away, we turned back to
　　look. Lightnin' was flashed all over the beach. Then we
　　saw the cross an'...

MAGGY: An' what?

ROB: An' there were...a shadow on the cross. But my sight
　　were so misty, I couldn't see clear enough to know
　　who...or what it was.

JED: I swear it was him. (*To MAGGY.*) Where you goin'?

MAGGY: Home. Where else?

VICAR: I trust you'll join us for Easter Communion.

MAGGY: Why should I?

VICAR: Well...among other reasons, to say a prayer of
　　thanksgiving that this nightmare is over.

JED: How d'you know it isn't just beginnin', Vicar?

MAGGY: No, it's finished. Joe wanted to free us from our
　　delusions. He wanted us to stand on our own flat feet.
　　An' if we have to pray to somethin' – like he said – let's
　　at least pray to our land, or the sea or the sky, or, God
　　help us, even ourselves. Anythin'! 'Instead of always
　　needin' someone to lean on, or to blame. Well, I am
　　willing to try it his way. So if the storm does blast the
　　village into the sea, it won't be the end of the world.
　　'Cause now I'm sure that I've still got enough spirit in
　　me to start a new life somewhere else.

SANDRA: I'll never forget him.

MAGGY: Nor will I. But I won't worship him, either. I don't
　　need him no more. I don't need anybody.
　　(*Mischievously she links her arm in ROB's.*)
　　'Cept perhaps you.

SIMON: What about the rest of us?

VICAR: (*Checking his watch.*) As it's almost time for
　　Communion, why don't the rest of you join me in
　　church?

JED: You'll find nothin' there. Only the ghost of what might have been. (*To ROB.*) Well, don't just stand there gawpin' at the waves. Take Maggy home. 'Least you've got someone to go home with.

SIMON: (*To BETH.*) Now don't cry, gal. Even though the Master's gone…you can always rely on me to eat your mussel pasties.

BETH: (*Gazing sea-ward and whispering in awe to JED.*) If you an' Rob didn't crucify the Master, then who's that.. on the water…walking towards us?

JED: It's the dawn, Beth. Only the sun can walk on water.

MAGGY: The rest's up to us. As always.

(*The sun has now risen, and it transforms the VILLAGERS into sunshine ghosts as they drift slowly away into the retreating mist, leaving the Sunken Cove shimmering in the white-gold light of dawn.*

BETH is the last one to go. Then – as if by an unseen hand – she is drawn back to look once more out to sea. At once she sees…)

BETH: O Master. Master…

(*Slow fade to blackout.*)

The End.